# PHILLIS

**UNIVERSITY OF CALGARY**
Press

# ❦ PHILLIS ❦

BY *Alison Clarke*

## A POETRY COLLECTION

Brave & Brilliant Series
ISSN 2371-7238 (Print) ISSN 2371-7246 (Online)

University of Calgary Press
2500 University Drive NW
Calgary, Alberta
Canada T2N 1N4
press.ucalgary.ca

LIBRARY AND ARCHIVES CANADA CATALOGUING IN PUBLICATION

Title: Phillis : a poetry collection / by Alison Clarke.
Names: Clarke, Alison, 1970- author.
Series: Brave & brilliant series ; no. 17.
Description: Series statement: Brave & brilliant series ; no. 17 | Includes bibliographical references.
Identifiers: Canadiana (print) 20200276344 | Canadiana (ebook) 20200276409 | ISBN 9781773851358 (softcover) | ISBN 9781773851365 (PDF) | ISBN 9781773851372 (EPUB) | ISBN 9781773851389 (Kindle)
Subjects: LCSH: Wheatley, Phillis, 1753-1784—Poetry. | LCSH: African American women poets—Poetry. | LCSH: Women slaves—United States—Poetry. | LCGFT: Poetry.
Classification: LCC PS8605.L37 P45 2020 | DDC C811/.6—dc23

The University of Calgary Press acknowledges the support of the Government of Alberta through the Alberta Media Fund for our publications. We acknowledge the financial support of the Government of Canada. We acknowledge the financial support of the Canada Council for the Arts for our publishing program.

Printed and bound in Canada by Marquis
This book is printed on Enviro Book Antique paper

Editing by Helen Hajnoczky
Cover images: Portrait of Phillis Wheatley, frontispiece from her book *Poems on Various Subjects, Religious and Moral*. London: A. Bell, 1773. The drawing of Phillis Wheatley was likely done by the Black artist Scipio Moorhead. Scipio Moorhead was a slave, owned by the Reverend John Moorhead, and the Reverend's wife Sarah gave Scipio art lessons. Colourbox 4253489 and 10403954.
Cover design, page design, and typesetting by Melina Cusano

*To Mom and Dad for their never-ending support,*

*and Conor who always believed.*

# CONTENTS

## PART I:
### Lector, Si Monumentum Requiris, Circumspice

## PART II:
## Fessos Tuto Placidissima Portu Accipit

## PART III:
## *Iter Sustinet*

# PART I

## Lector,
## Si Monumentum Requiris,
## Circumspice

# My Name Is~

My name, my name on this Earth is Phillis—the name from the ship that I was on. The Beast Of Death. I remember the people, the sailors uttering it. I remember like a mantra tainted with poison. Inside I flinch when that name was called, especially by my Master and Mistress. It's not easy, no, it is not easy. You get used to it, but not really, that pain, that gut flinch still remains, but I keep silent.

Now that I am on a new course that pulses through my veins, they say, The Ancestors say, "You are now Siptoraaki." Memories that seep through: like the sap of a tree. Flashes of Dreams run through the pathways of the brain: that collective co-mingling. So much was blocked out. So much was lost when I got on that ship. I think the Ancestors were protecting me, so I wouldn't Remember. It was too much. It Just    It was a gift, really, a way I could stay alive, so that I wouldn't be eaten out from my insides. So that the Pain would not cut me into two. Being on this ethereal plane, I remember in my mortal life, that sometimes, I felt like I was two people—the Phillis on the Earth, part of the mortal realm, that The Master and Mistress called upon, their model poet, artist, their "experiment" on display, their pet, and the other me—Griot, soothsayer, Teller Of Story, Daughter Of The Fulani, Keeper Of Secrets, Revealing Only what is necessary, keeping our Life, those private things, private. I think they took enough from us, they will not be privy to our private thoughts too. Mama knew this. She knew: "Reveal only what is necessary. Say only what is necessary. Your life with us, the stories, the coming together at the fire, the hearth, seeing the stars as the words fell out of our Elders' mouths, flying like the golden embers from the fire . . . Keep that for you, keep that in your heart, in that wooden chest, that is for you. It is enough. Allude to what you have lost, sing through your lays what you have lost, but those details, intimate, keep that for You, and you alone. You deserve that much. You are creating art so you can free your people. Do what you have to do, but don't give everything away. Keep that part for you, and for you alone. Yes, that is enough, my Daughter. It is enough."

# Chrysalis

*Lifeless In An Aquatic Tomb: that is how I felt, on this floating death trap, ship of oak, snow-tint sails shouting into the wind.*

The slaves were whipped—forced to—the music a macabre possession: seizures Of—The Dance . . . Exercise? Futile, too dehydrated, too hungry, fed once a day, if we were lucky . . . the food in buckets, people fighting for scraps, mush, and still in chains. The survival of the—no, the most lucky?

Shackled Africans beating on an Akan drum the patent rhythms of a neighbouring tribe whose land was all green-clad mountains . . . it was an internal hum, a pulsating beat resonance, of timeless time. Son of a chief, a gift, symbol that would reverberate, creating a troubling music. The ancestors nodded, hovering in a cloud of light: women, skin a light mahogany, or a deep mocha, dressed in bright clothing, fuchsia, indigo, gold and emerald. This music, The Drum, this haunting, an art form, but now: The Suffering . . .

The faces of the drummers—Masks: a convulsing, a mourning that could not be too horrifying, as the slavers would see, and more bodies would be hurled overboard. Feet, tension: like walking on fragments of glass, veins throbbing.

I want to pray, pay homage, while facing the rising sun, but I can't. The ones with blanched skin, I don't think they would understand. They might see it as an affront. I remember thinking this, even as a child. I remember. What was important was to Survive, and sometimes that meant great compromise.

The sludge, the waves of urine, feces, sweat, the STENCH As I walked, seesawing, in the bow of the ship, not steadily, for the element was turmoiled.

When I could climb to the deck, I witnessed Horrors that no child should see. Violations I still cannot speak of. A grotesque cavorting of bodies, a co-joining of limbs, male and female, forced together.

But the gyring slaves, chained together, was maddening, and the beating of the drum, the drum, preacher of our homeland Mother Africa, made pride seem torture. The Beauty, now mired, driven through the MUCK . . . What would mother and father say? I know what they would do: sob, slump, collapse, grasping onto silence, and look for escape, a way to kill, or a way to kill themselves. NOTHING will ever be the same.

I was taken, my Africa forsaken. My mother's cries, her crazed eyes, My father shrinking, shrivelling, bloody. NOTHING to be done. She was so helpless. And my father, if you could see, Something I never want to remember. And so—Here I am. On this ship for I know not where, but no place with warmth of the kind sun. There are no friends out here, and I don't know what to do. But the ancestors say: Do what you have to do: SURVIVE. You Are The CHOSEN ONE.

And You Must SURVIVE. The ode to the Morning Sun, A Pouring Out Of Water But that was useless. It didn't matter. It didn't keep me safe.

## Summer 1761: The Wharf

Months later . . . And now I am landed . . .
  And people with very bleached skin, hover about, in greater
                        numbers,
              Jabbering gibberish.
But I have a feeling that it won't last for long, I will soon know
              what they are saying.
     Strange words are being whispered. What bizarre sounds.
     What am I hearing? Voices from outside my head?
     "You must survive. You must. Go on."
     They are not being whispered from the white ones' lips.
     "Mama . . . Mama . . . What is in store for me?"
     "Do not be afraid my child," she whispered.
     "The ancestors are your backbone.
     You have no choice but to be strong."

And so here I am landed, this wooden whale has spit me out.
     To Remember What Was: A Cage. Butterfly Genesis
Will it give me life?
I don't know I just pray that things will get better. Will
they? The Chosen One . . . I don't know; I shiver: The air
freezes here; it's not like Home.

The sun, not like Home; it's frigid gold. I see a family before
me—near the wharf, I see a woman's grieving eyes. Has she
lost someone close? Has she lost a child, is looking for a child
to love? Or just a slave?
     I don't know, I close my eyes, and breathe . . .

7

# A New Life

Crash and burst of brush of sound, life, the seagulls, squalling, screeching . . . I am now on this wheeled carriage, that my family, and neighbouring tribes have talked about, seen, on the coast, and inland, gifts to Kings . . . The carriage was hauled by a horse, dust clouding my eyes, and then I look down, roads made out of stones, they look so smooth and round . . . Later, I learn that they are cobblestones, to help horses pace . . . I hear a distinct clip-clip, and continue to look around. As the journey continues, I keep hearing the same word: Boston. Is this where I am? The carriage stops. I breathe in heavily. I turn my head. The man and woman look at a house, a large brick one with huge white columns: I know they must have some kind of significance, but I don't know what. Spices drift pungent or sweet into my nose. I am ushered inside. The floors gleam a warm brown, and stairs lead upward to somewhere.

# Glimpses

I am hovering over the ethereal plane, and pictures, words, voices, rush through my head, like a flood, the pulsing of water . . . Ferocious in its intent . . . Streams becomes Rivers, become Oceans . . .

My words would be that papyrical lantern: my ideas ignited, the Ancestors tell me, catapulting a future abolitionist, Edmund Quincy, into action, often reading my work, with the shining encouragement of his grandmother; The Catalyst, the Bright Star—The Ancestors: their clothing long curves syncopation synergy a comfort—river banks, yet yearning    Possibility.

A cow of bronzy-gold appears, the habbanaya that is a gift to those, a symbol of good will and prosperity: the golden light that surrounds the cow reflects off her horns, and her soft moos comfort me . . .

I am at age eight, chalking words, on bedroom walls. Fresh from the floating tomb crossing The Middle Passage, The Horse Latitude, liquid graves of my people: no value a crying out for justice a crying out for home: screams in those waters, forever resounding—"Look, Mother, she writes. She is learning how to—how glorious!" Mary, the daughter of the Wheatleys, said with a smile. Nathaniel, her twin brother, was her mirror image: the only difference was their sex. The mother, Susannah, also looked pleased, and said, "I'll talk to your father, but I think—Phillis will be taught how to read and write. You will give instruction."

Susannah winked. "Yes, I think it is possible." The two flounced away in a flurry of skirts.

The ancestors nodded, murmured, chanted. They moaned, and the echoes sounded like a stick hitting a gourd full of water. They started to nod again, chanting now, in low tones, saying, "Remember What Is To Come—What Is To Come."

# Tempest

The Seas of Poseidon, howling, hurling curses: His domain,
Where mortals are merely flesh-clad corals.
I imagined seas, sky-high, the steep white foam
Quickly breaching the decks of the oak ship, the white sails
    bellying out,
Torn from the masts, the sailors screeching fears,
Messrs. Hussey and Coffin: eyes shocked, their faces rimed by
    the freezing spray
Of the sea about to gobble them up . . .

I listened to the ghastly tale of Messrs. Hussy and Coffin,
Two men from Nantucket who had barely reached shore,
To stay at my Master and Mistress in Boston, and were now in
    the living room.
The mantelpiece loomed behind them ominously, to prompt
    the tale.
Their ship had run into a hurricane off the coast of Cape Cod,
1766. I sat there, mesmerized, not far from the next table.
I sat at a table by myself, you see, apart from the Wheatleys.
But intently, I listened, as I knew my gift of writing would
    somehow
Help me escape this—

I closed my eyes, imagining the ship tempested like a child's
    toy,
Men clamouring to live—they scrambled into a lifeboat
Attached to the side of the ship. The boat was released,
    crashed, spilled,
Only a few men were able to flout the watery grave,
So Master Hussey thought of his future wife,

Betrothed, waiting for him, he saw her in an ivory white
    wedding dress,
That would set off her dreamy, rosy complexion,
The vision comforted him, even though the wedding was a
    year off.
Master Coffin also thought of his love, soon to be betrothed,
Her blue eyes, shining red hair, her beautiful laugh.
He shivered, trying to smile.
If he made it, if he did,
He would move up the wedding date,
And marry his love sooner. As for Master Hussey,
His nuptials were nigh, and he could hardly wait
To marry his maiden.

The Master and Mistress, the Wheatley family,
Knew the Coffins through Samuel Fitch,
A member of the New South Church,
And were intimates of that Christian community.
I went to Old South Church,
And I soon learned the comforting hymns,
They reminded me that I was Destiny's daughter,
And I was loved.
The vellum courted me. The Mistress thought me worthy
Of a journal bound in purple velvet, with gilt-edged pages of
    vellum.
I could feel the organic, the calf-skin made silk by grass.
I got my quill pen, dabbed it in the ink, and started crafting
    letters,
The soft turning of the pages as I wrote created a rhythm,
An aquatic wave of sound that mimicked the waves of the
    ocean:
I closed my eyes—
Solitude Is Language.
The moon, emissary of the goddess Diana,
Eyed my best work at night.

The moon was always my tutor,
And the female goddesses blessed my letters . . .

The Christian god, Jesus, was also worthy, but it was the Greek
    deities
That reminded me of the tales from home that explain all that
    is,
And explain why we act like we do.

This poem, my poem, about this tempest, appeared in
The Newport Mercury in 1767. I was 14 years old.
How capital my words' worth:
To witness my words imprinting paper.

# Prince

"Not next to 'My Phillis'!" I was sitting next to one of the slaves in the carriage. Prince was picking me up in the "Chaise" after a reading. One of his duties was as a valet or coachman. The horseman was at the front, and I was in the carriage, seated beside Prince, and looking out through the window: Stars, out, shining bright against a navy blue canvas, I wanted to talk to him, talk to one of my people, and we were having such a good conversation, my tongue felt free, and my heart, I didn't feel like such an island, I was able to reach out, and I felt good, and then—the Mistress said, "No!" The Mistress, said, "No!" She almost shouted, "If he hasn't the impudence to sit upon the same seat with 'My Phillis.' "

I always felt so cut off from everything from everyone. I just wanted to connect with someone like me, who looked like me, whose countenance resembled mine. I wanted to talk to someone who understood what we were going through, the masks we had to put on to hide what we were actually feeling inside—what we were really feeling. Often, I felt I had to act in pantomime, to hide the ghosts that lurked within, the pain within, the memories that seeped out, but I had to contain, in words, in readings, in the silence of my candlelit room, sitting at my desk. Or standing to look at the stars through the window. These moments, these stolen moments, Night was my friend, Night was my comfort, and The Story, it was always The Story that was my refuge against the storm.

# Library

I walked over, after getting out of the "Chaise," as Prince took me to the market earlier that day, and a tall man opened the door: there was a staircase, mahogany, curving toward the landing, ornate rugs and shining hardwood floors, the exterior red brick . . . It was the home of Mather Byles, nephew of Cotton Mather. Similar likeness, straight nose, brown eyes that don't miss a thing, he was a graduate of Harvard, the Cambridge of New-England I had lyricized. He had also been the librarian of the Harvard library, before he became a minister, just like his uncle.

"Hello, Phillis," Master Byles said, smiling. "Come in. It's wonderful to see you. I was looking forward to this visit. I have so much to show you." I entered the hallway, then turned right, and entered the room, following him. I gasped. Bookcases from floor to ceiling. So many towers of words bound up in paper, I almost cried. For books were always my friends, for their wordsmiths knew how to craft language, and make the linguistic sonorous.

"Here, Phillis," the former librarian said, smiling, "here are some of Pope's poems. There are a couple I would like you to see." He talked about one, a story in poetry form, an ode to epic poetry, where a woman was slighted, her honour in disrepute, and there was a battle between the mystical ones, fairies, which reminded me of the fairies they talked about in our stories, the elders mentioned them. How interesting.

Pope's language was musical, the visual, it took me to different worlds; Master Mather talked about heroic couplets, two lines that rhymed with each other. I had known that from what Mary, the Mistress's daughter, had told me. But I wanted to learn more.

"He translated the poems of Homer," he explained, "he knew Greek, and translated these words for future generations." Master Mather mentioned Jason, the Odyssey, and the Golden Fleece. I had heard about this mythology before, from what Mary had told me and the books she had given me to read. Here was the gateway, the Passage to the Mythic. The ancestors had told me. I saw their musical instruments in my mind's eye: flutes, of earthy browns and ivory, channeling reeds, bamboo, wood, and bone, the sound: a hush, an orchestra of tone, breathy swirls of air.

I think they are right. I must learn more. This is the way, the journey to my freedom. It will be the only way, and I mustn't waste time. I nodded.

Master Byles, who would be my guide on this Journey, read out some lines of Pope. He then showed me the letters the poet had sent, as they were in correspondence. He knew him. Pope did sound like a griot, not so much like my people, but still he was a storyteller.

I closed my eyes, and listened to the language.

This is it.

This is what I must do.

It is the beginning.

I will not tarry.

It is time.

# Odyssey

Pulsating Orb Of Light, The Moon doused in orangey gold dust:

She shines down, and hits my journal—gold embossed, vellum, it creates a flow, a streak of light, like lightning, I think of the Goddess of the Clouds, Blue, Purple, Rich Indigo, Violet, like the colours of my homeland, I remember what Master Byles said about Alexander Pope, he was Catholic, an outsider too, and his translations of The Odyssey, the Iliad, were his ticket, his passage to acceptance and financial stability. Would I ever achieve that? I thought about it for a moment, a meditation, a pulse . . . I felt . . .

I remembered the stories of Book XII, The Odyssey, Jason and his Argonauts, the quest for the Golden Fleece: setting sail for Colchis, on the Argo, the vessel flying across waters of cerulean, such a beautiful blue . . . Heading for . . .

The goddess of the clouds, Nephele, was desperate for a way to save her children, from the wrath of a jealous stepmother, the children, in the way, the children. She invoked a golden ram, gold-haired like the sun, with wings, to take the children to safety: To keep her daughter and son from harm—They rode on his back.

One child, the daughter, fell to her death, where she fell, now called Hellespont. Her brother made it to safety. And out of gratitude, he sacrificed the ram: In tribute to Zeus, the Saviour, King of the Gods, Supreme of them all on Mount Olympus. And now, the fleece of this Golden Ram was kept under guard, by a dragon, sleepless, murderous, eyes wide open: a haunting glow surged on, emanating from the pupils—from daylight to twilight and—

I think of the stories, of Odysseus who mentions Jason, I think of how stories echo, drum words through time. I know these stories that the Greeks told would shape my writing. The moon winks, as if in agreement. Yes, it is time. To dream out loud, to dream in rainbow ink that only comes with words, with the linguistic being a mirror, and this is how I must begin. This is how. Yes, this is how it begins. The moon continues to agree, shimmering waves of silver.

# It Begins

They talk to me: The Ancestors.
"Phillis, you are The One. Phillis You Are The Key."
Men, Women, appear again, surrounded by clouds of light,
hovering above me, they are robed
In rich colours: Crimson, Mustard, Bright White, Forest
Green.
I also see Indigo: swirling in the headdresses
And in the beadwork, in hexagonal jewellry
That reminds me of the Agades Cross,
Dreams Of Senegambia
A reminder of the balance, the Male and Female in
co-existence,
That gender should never be a cage, but neither should our
Afric heritage.
That's what the Ancestors tell me.
I must not forget.
Swirls of Amaranth, Tangerine, and Ebony surround the
Ancient Ones,
They are hovering in clouds of colour and light.
Their murmurs enchant like the rhythm of an Akan drum:
Echoing the heartbeat of West Africa
Their words are music,
An encouragement, a wave of love flowing into me.
My veins are vessels to their spiritual core.
They whisper.
They shout.
They send The Call, and the Spirits,
The Other ones, surround them, and sing, sing:

Allah is present, but in this world, in this Boston, Allah is
Lord.
He is guarding me, carefully,
For there is something I'm supposed to do,
It's to do with this book.
If I can get published,
Slap black print on white,
I will achieve freedom.

# The Old Colony House

I take a deep breath, and sigh . . . Sigh, for this is where I must prove that I wrote my verses, that I can architect lyrical song. I'm remembering, my mortal life, and it was early fall, 1772, in Boston, and leaves are downwards weaving, leaving paths of gold and crimson.

It's a red brick building, with statues of the Lion and the Unicorn, symbols of England, and Scotland, looking askance, near the roof. The Ancestors nod, this is where I must go.

One of the slaves, the domestic help from the Wheatley household, took me to where it would hopefully all begin. I stepped down from the carriage and prayed. I knew what I had to do, but I had to feel a sense of peace. A wave of serenity washed over me, but I still felt trepidatious, as I walked toward the Old Colony House, the fiery reds and golds of autumn swirling around me.

A tribunal, all albescent men, will decide if I'm a poetess or a fraud-ess. Some faces are famed, others not. I see Thomas Hutchinson, Governor of Massachusetts Bay, Mather Byles, a minister, and keeper of that beautiful and inspirational library, and my Master, John Wheatley.

I was scared, due to what is at stake—for if I can prove that the muse rolled off my tongue and into the pen, I have a chance to be free. Like Terence, the slave from Rome, who thanks to his proven intellect, and love of learning, was freed by his Master. Am I not worthy of Freedom? Will I be lucky enough to have the same destiny as Terence? The men of the tribunal are all seated at a table and I walked toward them. God was with me, and all of the angels. They would guide me to where I had to go, and in that instance, I wasn't afraid.

I pray that all these men will see these words were entrusted to me by Mnemosyne: Mother of the Muses, Goddess of Memory, a woman with jet black hair and eyes of fiery blue, shimmering like iced sapphire, hair streaming like the wind, may she, Mnemosyne, watch over me. May Mnemosyne's ethereal magic, through The Word, guide me, as well as God and Jesus, those of the highest, Father and Son who are at the helm. This is what I pray. My Ancestors, The Fulani, they will remember, not forget. My mother, still bowing, pouring out water, in dedication to The Sun: as it floats in the ocean of orangey-gold. In the realm of the goddess Aurora, where she presided over my homeland, Senegambia . . . emitting reverence, asking for protection, FOR ME.

I will divulge knowledge of poesy. Quote some poets. Recite some verses from various Shakespearean plays. Conjugate some Latin verbs. Convey my propensity for language. Then, I can publish my work, and start my exodus to freedom: like Terence who was freed by his Master, impressed by his intellectual achievements, language flowing out of his pen: forming plays, pieces that gave birth to laughter. His gifts were wings . . . and I have to show this, my artistic manifestation so I can be FREE.

Fire: The Ancestors, All Of Them, they Start to Dance, They
Start To Dance, it's Rhythm that I'm hearing. From the dawn,
from the Dawn of Time, the sky, the fiery tone, that Aurora
kissed, Stories have been told around the Fire. Fire is where
it all Began, the Light, to see, The Heat, to warm, the Heat to
cook, the Colour To bewitch, to be a spiritual link to the Other
World, connecting us to Our Ancestors . . .

To know the Stories, the Secrets of before, so we can listen
to them. To know, to Listen. To know. That's what they Say.
Learn from us, learn from our Mistakes, Learn from our
Triumphs, learn from our downfalls. This is the gift that we
give to you. This is The Gift. This is The Gift. Take it. And
pass on what you have learned to the next generation. My
songs, my lays, I will pass on to the next generation, but I
also pass it on to whoever will hear me, to hear my pleas, to
free my people, all of my people, so that we can carve out our
own Destinies, be able to reach for Possibility. I must do this
by appealing through Story, Mythology, which is a conduit
for uniting people, but also a Spark to Action, stronger than
appealing to someone's feelings of guilt.

I appeal to someone's Moral Compass as I did in my poem
about New Cambridge, to the young men who studied there,
the Future. I appealed from "Afric's seat" through Stories
familiar, that Pope referred to in his own work, especially
translating Homer.

I learn from those who guide me like Master Byles, talented,
and inspired by The Pen. This is the way—through Story,

through Narrative, through Dreams conjured by the
Egyptians, the Greeks, The Classics Of Story, through me
Swimming through a Sea of Latin, and other Languages to get
a sense, creating a world, a universe, that will connect readers
on a Journey of not only Delight and Wonder, but a lens to see
that shackling a part of humanity, enslaving a certain part of
humanity, The Afric, is wrong.

I must do it in a way that will not offend, that will not unleash
anger against me or my cause, but instead lend to man's
capacity for empathy, and the sense, a belief in Justice, For All.
That is my mission, that is my duty, being the "Ethiop." That is
why I am still here.

# What If?

What if Master Wheatley dies?
The Mistress has been sickly:
Fever-ravaged, violent shaking, Sweat, a liquid tomb . . .
Bloodletting, a tide of scarlet, futile at exorcising the demon
that is illness
Sheets soaked, a foreboding stink of death,
And the coughs, oh the coughs, that rack her body as she
gasps . . .
Her Eyes:
The light wearing thin;
What of me when she dies?
She wanted to be my mother, because of the child she lost.
But she's not my mother, she is across the seas,
And I probably will never see her again.
She wants to protect me,
That is why she is allowing this educational and creative path.
But she isn't protecting me, I'm still a slave.
And this foundation of sand, it will all fall away when she is
gone.
My "position"?
Another slave master, another doubtful future,
Precipitous, hanging in the balance . . .
I have to fight for my freedom,
and the only way is through Story, in Poetry.
The mists rose from the shore,
And I see Them,
THE ANCESTORS
The Fulani tribe:
They are calling.

I hear them.
The words, different tongues, a meditative pulse;
And I feel like I'm at home.
The harp, the kora,
Sounds like wind-strummed lyres,
The harmonics chiming like church bells,
An instrument, carved out of calabash,
Covered with the skin of the gifted sow,
The sounds of home soothe me, they sustain me.
They say: "Hold on."
When she was recovered, Mistress Wheatley contacted the
newspapers in April 1773
About my casting off . . .
To meet my patron, the Countess of Huntingdon, to meet
others who will encourage my work,
reaching for the mantel, subscriptions for my impending
publication.
A poem heralds my voyage
My departure from America
To that other world
Across the aquatic lair
They know me,
The Britons,
My work,
Poems published in newspapers,
They hopefully will greet me,
Another gateway opening:

And continue to be the portal that I seek
So that pages of poetry become my Emancipation
Proclamation.

# Mother

Mother of the Muses
Mnemosyne,
On the Open Shore
Here I am . . . To receive your lore.
I am shipping out with Captain Robert Calef,
And Nathaniel, son of Master Wheatley.
I will be singing my lays in Britannia,
So much has to be orchestrated,
and I am one note among many.
The ship, the London Packet, is weighing anchor,
For the realm literary,
England,
May 1773.
The wind, the zephyr,
And his daughter, whispered in my ear:
Listen, Wait.
LISTEN.
I closed my eyes:
A ball of Light, dragging across the sky,
Leaves a path
Of fiery gold against the azure ground.
The chariot, going slow, but surging in brilliance . . .
Mother Mnemosyne, riding gloriously,
Her chariot powered by dreams, images,
Memories, visual stories . . .
Imaginings, tellings,
Of what COULD Be . . .
But what is really To COME?
The One With Eyes of—

A force kicked up from Zephyr's Daughter's breath.
Aurora then emerges from the shadows, sceptre in her hand,
The ball of flames, satiating the sky:
Track the path of fire.
But the chariot disappears, and so does Aurora,
And the Mother of The Muses seems to be mid-air aloft,
But then a horse, a horse of white appears: He has wings.
She rides him, following the gilded way, until the ball turns
white gold.
She disappears. She reappears when the shadows shift to
branches,
Tossing in the wind, arms of night,
The ebony, friendly, becoming velvet ocean, and a segue of
silver,
Then an orb, a mother of pearl that now traverses the aerial
layer,
I continue to close my eyes:
Mother Mnemosyne, gift me with articulation,
That I may convince those that I am thy worthy comrade,
Your gifts, so that there will be those who will honour my
work,
My book-to-be fetched from dreams,
Hopes and memories manifesting in black ink,
The pages, an ivory chapel,
And the words ebony pews.
For I must recite some of my poetry
to intrigue future patrons with my impending publication.
Gift me with the power of your daughters:
Especially the siren of poetry, so that my recollection, my
recitation,
Of words emblazoned by Pope, Shakespeare, and Sappho will
echo and reverberate
Sonorous, unforgettable tones to the ears,
The palate of sound
Make me your tenth daughter,

Goddess Of Ancestral Memory,
Orchestrating Beauty through Word, Image, and Sound
Let me be the harp on which you play,
So that my song may make those weep with tears of jubilation.
I silently mouthed these words,
But they were not silent,
But waves of Prayer, Hope,
A kneeling on a star, looking up into the heavens:
A tapestry of colour, a dark cerulean,
Swirls of fuchsia and orange,
Fiery champagne, unforgettable violets,
Merging into a crescendo
Of emerald, gold, and vermilion.

# Voyage

At Death's Door: the Screams, the Screams . . . I remember.
But now, sailing on The London Packet, Venus is wooing the
Moon, wooing Diana, some say, and so I see the Celestial
Dance. It's a new voyage, from the ashes, the Phoenix does
rise. I told the Master and Mistress about my mother, a vivid
memory, the Magic of the Sun, the Creator, captured by my
pen in poems like "An Hymn To The Morning," and the
ancestors nodded—Synergy, Synergy, that's what they said:
ode to the Sun, ode to my Culture, the Fulani.

From the ashes, the ashes, we often have to transform . . .
start again a foundation, making it anew: from the sorrowful
sounds, that music on the ship, they say it'll morph into a new
music form . . . that will belie what we have been through,
a bird of song, but one that wails, the suffering made into
something to be listened to, an art form whose genesis is
pain. We have done this so many times in memoriam . . .

This voyage on The Packet is an Emergence from—because I
now sail on a ship to discovery, sailing on Dreams, and I hope
Opportunity, but reminds me of another journey on a similar
vessel, Aquatic, but one that carried human cargo. I'm sure
I'll see in Londinium, ships with passengers that will unite
loved ones, that transport those from one part of the world to
another for pleasure, work, family, but I remember those other
vessels, those of Death. We don't forget these things, and then
I looked into Captain Calef's eyes, I saw that he Saw, and knew
what I was thinking. I was remembering.

When I wrote about Messrs. Hussey and Coffin, I purposely focussed on what they went through, their hardship. I did not write about mine. It was too hard to write about, and I never will write about what I went through on that ship. I will never write about the deaths, the whips, those who threw themselves overboard rather than deal with what was lying ahead, the inevitable. There are those who will look at my poetry and wonder why I didn't write about this, why I didn't write specifically about my Homeland, why I didn't write more about my parents, the former life. It's too painful.

Why write about a life that was ripped from you? I can't. I won't. I deal, I sleep with enough ghosts hanging about me. I sleep with too many screams, sounds of cries, hopelessness. I sleep with the dead, seeing their bodies sink slowly to the bottom of the ocean, descending down the aquatic steps, and whose carnage is food for the sharks. They tell me. They tell me. These Stories travel. William Bosman, he knew, the movement of sharks following those ships of Death: *A New And Accurate Description Of Guinea* . . . and I have read so much in that last lifetime: It's enough to sleep with the Suffering of The Dead, I do not need to relive it in my waking dreams in my Waking Life. It is Enough. C'est Suffit. It Is Enough.

## Two

Currents Of Consciousness Are Coming Back . . .
Sinews Of Memory: Being Siptoraaki;
Currents of experiences, images continue to wash over me.
I remember sailing on The London Packet, with the Captain
who was the engine:
Robert Calef who had connected in December 1772 with
Archibald Bell,
My future publisher,
And now, to expand the Journey, to read my work,
And reaching those who would be interested in my Story, The
Poems . . .
We should be reaching Britannia in June of 1773
As my ancestors tell me . . .
"So Phillis, you must be excited."
"Yes, sir," I answered. "It is a great opportunity."
"Yes, it is, but one you are very much aware of. Yes, I am
happy to have connected you to Archibald.
Your work is excellent, and you'll go far. I have had the good
fortune to be at one of your
readings. The Wheatleys are gracious hosts." I nodded in
response.
I walked toward one side of the ship, and looked out to sea. It
was relatively calm, unlike
The tempest that Messrs. Hussey and Coffin experienced.
I shivered: I hope that never happens to me. I then stopped to
think.
Robert Calef, the captain, his eyes, mirrors:
Reflecting what we should all see, but don't.
Observance, knowing of the Middle Passage:

Torn from our homeland, then landing in America.
Yes, the captain's eyes are reflecting the reality of my people,
The unspoken that needs to be spoken:
Which is why I am determined to see it through,
The Publication Of My Poems.
A Written Plea to end this Disease.
Injustice, another lens—
But there are those who shield their eyes,
Like how they shield them from the bright sun,
The truth can be a ball of blazing fire,
And those who do not want to see will veil their eyes.
I remember The Boston authorities "told the Constable of the
Watch
'To take up all Negroes Indians and Molatto Slaves,
That they may be absent from their Masters Houses,
After 9 O'clock at Night,
Unless they can give a good and satisfactory Account
Of their business.'"
But I have to think of the people that are helping me to
publish these poems:
This is how I survive.
This is how I continue to Forge The Path,
With the Ancestors, the Angels, God and Jesus at my side.
In my mind's eye, I remember:
The Countess of Huntingdon, my mistress Susannah Wheatley,
Captain Robert Calef, and I think of Archibald Bell, my future
publisher,
surrounded by his lair of books,
Companions manifest in vellum—
The volumes of ink-painted words.
An art form undervalued,
But Mother Mnemosyne understands,
I see my Future Publisher dressed in velvet, a triangular hat,
Breeches, shirt open at the neck, looking at his printing press,
Knowing what has to be done . . .

P

Princess.

Is that what

Nathaniel wanted to

Find?   A Princess . . .

In London Towne?

A          Lady       Waiting

That would grace His Presence

At His Manse?

A House, given to Him by His Father, Or One He would
Purchase on His own?

To have that kind of Opportunity:

It's a net through which a seashell can disappear.

# What Awaits?

What will I see when I get to those shores?
I see my people in the morning sun,
Their feet bound in leather, with bright buckles,
Making sharp, staccato sounds against the cobblestone
And at night, candlelight creating warm hues from their velvet
jackets, and hats,
The women wearing petticoats, dresses, with tiny waists,
Blossoming out into moving bell shapes of the finest cloth
Hair, jet black, covered with fashionable bonnets trimmed
with lace,
A whole community, that this Fula could embrace,
A community safe, because of a decision, Somerset v Stewart,
Making England a safe haven
Freed people—never being returned to the evils of slavery . . .
A peaceful and comforting meditation,
Orchestrated like a violin,
The musicians,
Granville Sharp, and other abolitionists,
Who use their voices as swords, to cut through the evil, that
darkness, that sin.
I could be a part of this.
Obour, Sister In Spirit, Slave, My Only Friend, said: "Stay. Do
not come back."
Am I meant to stay here? Would I fare well here?
I have heard that James Albert Ukasaw Gronniosaw,
Another author, an "Afric Muse,"
A Kindred Spirit In The Word, who penned his Life Story, is
living here, and doing fine.
He is not rich, but he is able to lead some kind of life,

in dignity, with a community that looks out for him.
This isle,
People who are sympathetic to our cause
Another reason that I eagerly cross this threshold:
They could help me attain my Freedom.
The Ancestors again nod, swirls of colour surround them:
A        VORTEX
I    am    Immersed   IN
They say: "Yes, Phillis, this is the way, this is the portal,
Your words, your gifts are the Light, open that door,
Mother Mnemosyne, Mother of the Muses,
And The One who pushed you out from her womb,
She is also here with you in spirit,
She is the warm feeling pulsing through your veins,
Remember,
don't forget,
REMEMBER . . . "

## Are You?

"Phillis, are you excited?" asked Nathaniel, with a smile.
"You will be the first—the first black woman to—"

A sudden blast of wind cut out the remaining words,
As if Zephyr's daughter already knew them,
The thoughts already bruited on the breeze.

"Yes, you will be."

The Captain, Robert Calef, smiled at me.
No, not all are evil—
Not all harbour the darkness . . .
Doing the work of the—
Not all.

The sea mist surrounds me,
The salty air kisses my cheek . , .
Kisses,
Kisses.
Yes.
Yes.
The goddess of the sea,
Daughter of Poseidon,
Kisses it,
And she smiles,
I smile,
More fortune will come upon me
Like Rain.

# Crossing Over—June 1773

It's a month later, and now we have entered the gates of Britannia with Captain Robert Calef as our Nautical guide. There was an apartment waiting for us in London, and there were many visitors, including Benjamin Franklin, an admirer of my work. It felt good, a relief, and a joy to talk about writing, art, poetry. I am seen as an artist, a literary one, and that is a victory.

But what I also saw—another genesis of living, breathing art—architecture and these creators crossing over into both art and science; It was a delight to behold, and the science of looking at the movement of the stars, and measuring time: to create longitude, to stop the sinking of so many ships. The Royal Observatory, it reminded me about my ponderings on the universe, in my poem, "Thoughts On The Works Of Providence:" " . . . which round the sun revolves this vast machine," and "Ador'd the God that whirls surrounding spheres . . . " In my other life, the Fulani were passionate about astronomy, mathematics; the wheels keep turning, and the currents of memory wash forth, and break through, like water bursting through a dam; The torrents are coming forth, and I recall . . .

# Londinium

As I walked these grounds, and others, seeing the Greenwich Hospital, the Blue Towers Of Navigation, overlooking the Thames, one—the circumscribing of Time, the other a compass for ships . . . This is what I remember:

Wings . . . metallic, I see . . . flaming gold . . .

Two towers    Blue domes   One calling to the ships, the compass, the harbinger—

The other Father Time, A Clock.

I walked down the stairs

Between the columns

I saw the face of a woman

Red        brick . . .

I dove into oceans of colour, the Painted Hall:

Thornhill was the Captain of the seas of Colour,

I looked around the Naval Hospital, The Royal Hospital For Seamen At Greenwich;

It called to me, and so did the Royal Observatory:

Carving time from the Stellar, The Celestial Globes Of Light—

The Star Room: 1676, Francis Place, I thought of the men from that engraving, one looking through a telescope, looking at the stars; Using the Celestial to Create Time.

This Voyage, so transformative, I can have a new start. I have made friends here; Granville Sharp comes to mind: the architect of Somerset, the decision that gave my people freedom if they escaped to the shores of Britannia.

A mighty, but reassuring call. She Said, Obour Said, "Stay. Don't Come Back. You have a gift. Don't come Back. Don't—

I have a feeling that I will not be able to. Unlike James Albert, and others, I will not be able to make the lair that surrounds the Thames home. But I feel the shift here. I could create a life here, based on my words. It is more than Possible.

But what is meant to be, will be. We all make choices, have to make choices, but I feel as a woman, an Afric, we have less choices than others. But I see, and going around this towne, London Towne, I do see: So much can spring from the Imagination, so much that shows me that Art is important, us artisans of The Word, we are important, papyrical monuments for those who lift the page. These gifts can create openings. Gateways, portals into something New, to be a key in rebuilding a life. What Obour told me; And This Architect, Sir Christopher Wren, reminds me of this. He who designed St. Paul's Cathedral, and the Greenwich Hospital, sitting by the Thames. The Royal Observatory, not far, surrounded by Green, Green, Green, and A Statue of King George II stands guard before the new buildings.

This hospital that is an ode to Queen Mary II, Queen, wife, to King William III. Her Dream to pay tribute and take care of sailors like the ones that fought the great Marine Battle of La Hogue in 1692.    To take care of those who sacrificed their lives.

This architect, Christopher Wren, an artist, his work immortal, standing tall for all time. I remember standing directly under the dome in St. Paul's, looking down at the circle of black marble in the floor: Si monumentum requiris, circumspice.

My mind whirls, the wheels spinning faster.

Water can be a Healer, The Sea can be a Healer . . . But it also can be A harbinger Of Death . . . So many Stories . . .

This Journey, I am Taking things back: making something new from the ashes. I am the Phoenix: taking the pain, and remaking it, creating something else—From the birthing of pain, the screams on that ship, to something else.

Now, the Sea, crossing Her Again, is now a vessel of opportunity, a Dream built on the lyric music, my lays, the cry of freedom for my people, but I had to take a step, take the journey to Britannia to make it happen.

Walking down the steps, the columns · More    Story    I Remember    Walking    Along The    Thames    Listening to the    Lapping    Of    The    Waves    Hyde Park, So Much Magic, Freedom Around Me    The Decision    Somerset    a place for slaves to shuffle off those coils and grasp Freedom. That    could    be    me

Obour said, "Stay, where you have a chance. Stay. You—You—"

The Ancestors Speak Loudly: You Must Do What Is Right For You. You must . . . You Must . . .

But I feel an obligation to Mistress Wheatley. She opened up the Floodgates to my Emancipation, my Future Emancipation, I feel I want to stay, in Londinium, but I feel an Obligation. An Obligation that Obour doesn't understand. I remind her, Mistress Wheatley of the One she has lost. In some strange way, I know it doesn't make sense. But, there it is. I could stay. The precedence is there: Somerset. But I still feel—

Boston is not home. Where I can sculpt with The Word, that is home, and that is anywhere; I am not limited to Borders, NO. There are No Limits. That is what I know, I am standing in front of the Thames at The Riverside, the bank. England is a way out, and I think of James Albert Ukasaw Gronniosaw.

He is free here. So close, but so far. I don't think I'll get a chance to see him. I think that's not possible. But what is possible is my Freedom.

I know it'll still be a battle, but there it is—a chance to be something more. To do something more, to have a better life. I Have To TRY. I Have TO.

The Ancestors whisper to me: "It won't be long now. Soon, you'll be coming home." I remember this moment, that moment, as I am Now Memory, Siptoraaki, above The Clouds. I am now with all my Sisters and Brothers and Looking Down at That Moment. Signposts, years are just signposts, it's the Memories themselves that Loom Large.

The Fulani is full in me now, but I still remember the Other Life. I am a Fusion of things, even now, and that is also a Victory. They can't take that away from me.

It is in my writings, it is in me. The Reverence, Bowing down to the Sun, Pouring Water, Respect For Nature's Elements: The Magical, The Meditation, The Solar, The Aquatic, Story As Language, emanating from my Fulani culture like the roots of the tree—Lekki; so Powerful that Words have Wings. Faeries, black faeries, we have them in the Fulani, we are a people that travel wide, and so Stories Carry. This realm that is the Fulani. Yes, she Reverberates, she does, and the synchronicity with the storytellers like Pope, Homer, Shakespeare, Sappho, and others. We Remember. And there is more to come.

As I wrote to Obour later, "I can't say but my voyage to England has conduced to the recovery (in a great measure) of my Health. The friends I found there among the Nobility and Gentry. Their benevolent conduct towards me, the unexpected, and unmerited civility and Complaisance with which I was treated by all, fills me with astonishment, I can scarcely Realize it."

I had never felt that kind of respect before. In Londinium, they saw me for my gifts, not for the colour of my skin. I was an artist, not a slave. Not Something lesser than. I was a human being. That had a right to a life, to be able to start a destiny of my own, a destiny that I should not have to beg for. This is what I know. That was the shift. I will never forget that. I never will.

# Susannah

The Mistress Susannah,
back on the alien shore, where I first landed.
She believes in me:
Is it because I am the daughter that she had lost?
The daughter she bore before Mary?
The one who had died when the twins were nine years of age?
Was I her replacement?
Her surrogate?
Dreams wished to be fulfilled, but were not in an earlier time?
Her first daughter,
Did she have her eyes?
Her laugh?
Her smile?
Did she make the corners of my Mistress's mouth curve up
Ever so slightly, In Those Quiet Moments?
Somehow, I believe, I do the same for her . . . in some strange
way,
Daughter Of The Fulani, from another land,
Slave,
But somehow I am her.
I have fulfilled that role.
But I must break free
That Bond—
Plaster That Must Be Shattered
For me to truly

Have Agency:
Freedom.

# she

My mother would have been proud.
I miss her dearly.
I miss her laugh, her smile,
Her love, an aura of Light, and unconditional acceptance,
It surrounded me, and kept me safe.
But that wasn't for long, and the darkness penetrated this
elusive fortress:
Ripples of Water        Resurfacing
And    I      Remember
Mama:
I knew I was your entire world.
But now, that's gone,
And all I have are ghosts,
That is all,
My other legacy,
Besides my words;
But Mama,
I      thrive,
Despite being left in a desert.
I         THRIVE.
I am writing,
Riding oceans of possibility,
Words are the mast,
And Imagination blows upon the sails
Words are song,
A lyrical music
I look up as the Moon looks down on me,
Glowing brighter,
As    if    in    response,

Continuing to pulsate
Undulations of midnight blue.

# Book: September, 1773

Emblazoned with light, the words ignite the page. The
Moon, a silver pendulum. I cry. This work, that began with the
first poem being published in 1767, I was fourteen years old.
The tale of Messrs. Hussey and Coffin comes to my mind, and
their encounter with the Cape Cod tempest. And now—My
mother would have been proud. My father . . . I am a griot,
what they always imagined, as I had always loved magic in
story, and listened to the elders around the fire, as they told
us about our ancestors, and those who lived among the stars.
I remember. And now, look. Mama, Papa, I did it. I made it.
And now, because of these gifts, being the Griot, and having a
published book, I am free. Anything is possible. Mama, Papa,
I am free.

# Freedom

"Here it is, Phillis," my Master says, "here it is. The solicitor has drawn up the papers. I have signed them." I sit across from my Master's desk made out of mahogany. This is the study, with bookcases all around, a Persian rug, and walls of shining oak.

A grandfather clock ticks away in the distance. "It's your time," it says. "It's your time Seize it, savour this moment, for there won't be another one like it."

Here I am, white linen cap on my head, plain white dress, simple petticoat. It is fall again, and I remember going to Old Colony House—about a year ago. Things are coming full circle. One journey has ended, and another has begun. Crimson and gold swirl around outside the window. Yes, Yes, it has happened, and a light shoots into the room, a ray of golden Light. Yes, It Is Time. Soon after my words became wings after entering the gates of Britannia. Meditations are rivers. I have achieved what the Ancestors wanted, predicted, they spoke to me in dreams: swashes of colour, they told me my time was coming, and to celebrate. I asked them what was ahead. There was silence. But inside me I knew, things might be hard, things will never be the same.

But at least, I am free, and that is a start for my people. For we all have to start somewhere: To Carve out our Dreams, A Liturgy of Narrative — To Etch in the AIR What we see.

# John

I met him on Queen Street, selling fruits and vegetables. He
smiled at me. I smiled back, and walked back towards the
Master's house, as the Mistress was sickly. The dust in the
streets getting on the clothes, and the heat, I immediately had
to seek shade.

Sometimes I saw him, white wig, cane, neck decorated with
a lacy collar. Other times, triangular hat, velvet jacket and
breeches. I wasn't sure: who was this man? He seemed to have
many masks. We talked, often, off and on. He was trying to fit
into this society, and as a free black man it wasn't easy. But he
didn't give up hope, and that's what I saw.

We married in November 1778, ceremony where we jumped
over the broom, a new Beginning. Our first child was born
in 1778, and the second in 1779. It's been a struggle ever since,
but I have hope, it's the only beacon I can hold on to. I have
no choice. If not, all is lost. The dreaming is important,
imagination . . . it's forever swimming in my memory, the
stories my elders told me,  my Fulani tribe, in Senegambia.

Well, I'm in a new land now, and I must adjust, and continue
to make that shift. The old life is over. I close my eyes and
pray. May God and Jesus get me through this one. With the
father and son from up above, these are the things that keep
me going.

I sit by the window of a house in Wilmington, a shack really,
where we went after Boston had been under siege: The
American Revolution—Military men from New-England had
barred the movement by land of the British Army. I sigh. The

house, dilapidated, dirty, I was isolated, in the countryside, not knowing a soul. I had so many dreams. I sit and wait. Sit and wait.

# Star

Star of Orion: The picture, glistened on the baby rattle, I used it, to soothe him to sleep, baby with a small nose, mahogany eyes, mocha skin, and soft, black, curly hair. The rattle was a gift from Obour Tanner, my only true friend, my only black friend: a Sister conjoined in Kismet, who came upon this shore, taken from our homeland, just like me.

This life, working, as a scullery maid, trying to write, having children, Death often being a Harbinger, I felt like I was living in a sanctuary of mist, and John . . . away so often, one of the few cherished friends I could trust, who understood was Obour. And having just the One, is all you need. You don't need a friendship with many, all you need is just the one. And I am so lucky to have that, it's such a Gift.

Given a good education, we were doing only what we can, vying for the unattainable Golden Fleece; I looked at my child, he was peaceful now, sleeping in a bare room. It was quite cold here—not enough logs to keep us warm, my husband was out, working odd jobs, doing what he can do. I clean, a few seamstress jobs . . . Only a bed for me and John, a crib for the baby, our first child had already died . . .

There is a morgue-like tone to the room: It's quiet. Quiet. It's 1779 and I wrote a poem, Mr. and Mrs.—talking about a child nearing the—God and Jesus at the throne, the child being welcomed . . . and I know the child in my poem will be my son, the second damned by the disease that is poverty.

The sun filtered through the window with no drapes. When I can I cover it with some linen. I hear the Ancestors loudly, and I see their colours: red, yellow, green, and white. They speak to me, and give me comfort.

Everything is connected, the dead, the living, we are all connected: the celestial, the spiritual, the heavens, and here on earth, there is a bridge, it is a force, nothing is separate. I remember, and the Ancestors say: "Hold on." So I must—not only for myself, but for this little one . . . Yes, I must hold on.

# Refuge

The Mystics call to me . . . call, call, the columns, Doric,
colonial architecture, but harkening back to a different time.
I think about Pope, I think about Homer, Socrates; I think
about Terence, the Greeks, Me, holding the hand of Chronos:
Traversing Epochs, seeing footprints left by Proteus. My
children, very sick, poorly, my husband is away, trying to
provide for us, but to no avail, nothing is falling into place.
It's a struggle, a constant struggle.

We are here: my two sons, with Mistress Elizabeth Walcutt,
niece of Mistress Wheatley, who saw something in me, but
now has entered another realm, leaving the earthly plane in
March of 1774. I will never forget it. It's now 1780, and I am
here, in the niece's house, for my husband is often out, trying
to find work, and I am with the children. The poverty sucks
whatever vitality they have, I have; Elizabeth has been kind,
letting us stay here, to regain our health, our well-being, trying
to retain our humanity among the squalor of subsistence. It is
not easy.

She runs a school, for young children, ABC's, slates, writing
numbers, letters in bright white chalk, which reminds me of
when I started writing letters, copied from the Bible, on walls
in a bedroom, I know that the Ancestors saw this. They did
see. Now, I see the Mistress singing nursery rhymes, telling
stories, an easy way to a child's mind, and imagination, the
gateway to learning, but not enough people see . . .

But these children are learning, easily, and it's no wonder the
Mistress is so enthusiastic. I wanted to teach, give people my

knowledge through The Word, siphoning off the linguistic, which is the portal to retention, to memory; I wanted to—I look at my children, therein I See—But what life will they have? Poverty is the mother of missed opportunities. I look at my babies, their soft skin gleaming in the light, and—it's not enough to be free, there must be opportunity for us, and when will that time come? I don't know. My husband is trying, a grocer on Queen Street. He squeezes out a living, selling fruits and vegetables, sometimes meat, as it is a rare commodity, and even rarer now, nearing the end of the Revolutionary War.

This house a victim, gun blasts, cannons, but the columns still gleaming white, as if harking back to a past life . . . We will be here for six weeks . . . I Battle: Trying to find a sense of Peace.

# Mary

She Believed in my gifts, circle of books around her, a circle of silk, her dress. She sat at the desk: Latin, Greek became familiar friends. I wondered what she had thought about me, about this, a young Ethiop in this land, this Boston. It was a request from her mother, to tutor me, she didn't have a choice, but I think she enjoyed teaching, I remembered her smiles, and her laughs, the mirth in her eyes . . . But for some reason, she didn't train as a teacher. I often wondered. These things, these questions surfaced, in that life, the terrestrial one, and in this present one, as a being surfing the celestial plane.

Yes, Mary wanted to be a teacher, but later on, she would do well, marrying Reverend John Lathrop of Old North Church. She would go on to have children, and two would grasp adulthood. But she died young, a couple of years ago, at 35 years of age . . . from childbearing. There was a price for being Female: Marriage the only option, a stable shelter, but for those of a sable countenance . . . I remembered the struggling cry of my two young ones, staying at the home of Elizabeth Walcutt. I remembered Mary, closing my eyes, and what surrounded me was silence.

# N

Nebula: What   Was   What  will  BE—Fire, Memory, Loss,
Gain, Dreams,
                    Graveyards of—
I hear The Cries, and I'm drowning: the water, I try To Tread;
Try to  drown  Them  Out  Sinking  deeper  into   a
Whirlpool   The Abyss of Longing   The   Memories,
The   return  to   Memory:  Rivets  From  My  Brain
Silence which isn't Silence, Pain which is not Pain, because
I Am NUMB. I Feel   but  I  Don't   I See   I Know
But — Confusion,

Quicksand:
I grab,  Try  to   but to No Avail, and I can't See  Blind
but  Somehow  I  Know  what to  do,  Hold On, Hold
On  TO   do Not Sink , Try Not to, and I wonder For How
Much Longer . . . The Sirens Rage, Eyes Alight: Lightning
becomes swords, daggers, and
I double Over—The Thrust . . .

# PART II

## Fessos Tuto Placidissima Portu Accipit

# The Future—Part I

Flights of Fancy, surge of Cerulean . . . Liquid thought,
dripping onto paper . . . I worked, worked, in twilight, in
candlelight, Mother Mnemosyne and all her daughters around
me, especially her daughter, Calliope, it was an experience,
it was a song, frenetic, kinetic, an experience without words.
That was that moment, nothing else. It was always about    The
Work
But later, after it is all done, you just don't know, you just
don't know what kind of impact    you    will    have    The
reader, the observer, the one who dives into your words,  you
just don't know    not quite    not quite    And to see, to
hear, of others who are inspired, influenced by your Path; It is
rewarding . . . and in this life, this celestial life as Siptoraaki,
I know the impact,  the collective consciousness; I already
know; we are all connected, the stars in the universe:  the tree
with    many    roots    Lekki. Not just making contact with the
ground, but are in connection, communication with other
trees, why are we humans so different?
And so, I fly, fly through time, swim in the cosmos, sliding on
the Milky Way, the shooting stars,  I glide, riding this mystical
harmony, the constellations, everything twinkling symphony,
and then I descend:  Down    Down    Down    to the Earthly
plane, the terrestrial realm, I forge forward through time—
The Future. To hear, see, those who I have shaped, their lives
like river beds birthed by stone, sand, and sediment. The
Spirit, coursing through our souls rivers of symbiotic thought.
That is what I know, So I go forward, swimming through
time, to hear what they have to say, hear their thoughts, their
ponderings, as we are all part of the Collective Consciousness,

the Ancestors know, have known before the Beginning: Me,
a Time traveler, Siptoraaki, a Time Traveler, crossing the
Cosmos, to know that my work, my life was not in vain: Yes.
To see, to know, to Hear, To feel, To understand, and To Be At
PEACE.

# Harriet Tubman: 1859

I am sitting in my home, wooden frame, a kindness, a great kindness, from the Senator, Senator Sewell, My parents safe: Older, wrinkles, dark skin toughened by memory, toughened, by What They Had Seen . . . But I will be on a new Journey, to help out, be a soldier, to continue the Battle during the Civil War . . . but before I go, dreams come to me, Dreams, And Thoughts Of What Was, What is, and What I am, it is a circle, it is continous, one hand feeds another . . . And  they  are Resurfacing Yes, They Are:

Black Man to be beaten—teetering near Death—I said NO Put Myself in front of him: A BARRICADE, The Overseer, his eyes made mad with anger, seering into me, a two pound weight thrown at me; I was never the same; At any time falling into a deep sleep, but it was also a Gateway to Dreams—Prophetic Dreams.

I escaped in September, 1849, with just the clothes on my back, me and my brothers, I propelled myself, the spirituals chiming, ringing, in my head, the North Star was overhead, and Jesus was my Protector:  Afraid?  A bit, but I   kept Going  I knew.  KNEW.     KNEW.  The first time: My brothers, they had to go back. They were afraid, and the bounty on my Head . . .  But, the second time, I persevered, and The Archangel, Michael was with me, I saw his sword glowing.  TIME.    TIME.   TIME.    IT Ticks.  they Say I will Be I will Be: The MOSES They Whisper.   Moses.     The Ancestors  The Ashanti, They were known to be Warriors: Streams Of Colour Before Me; Streams of Colour, Blue, purple, gold, draped over their shoulders, an aura of

light surrounded them: Men, Women. Yes, So there Will
Be A Battle    Yes    They Whisper, They Shout, They
Dance.    Keep Going, Child, Keep Going. Up Through
Pennsylvania, into Philadelphia: Up, Up, You Will Be Free,
And Then, Get Your Niece, Her Children, You are a Part Of
a – We are all Connected.   Yes   Yes   And it will continue, so
many will depend on your guidance and knowledge.

You have remade yourself, Now, You are Harriet, but we'll
always  remember your beginnings: Araminta  Araminta
You will Rise RISE RISE   Your   People   Take Hold, Grasp,
That Ring, The Brass One, and Lead Your People. There was
one before you, a Griot, who helped her people through the
Word, and now, you will be the General.  It Is Time. I heard
them chanting.  It Is Time.  I heard them Singing. It is
Time . . . they were Stomping Their feet:


Child


It  is—

# Blessings: 1911

And now I am in a room, surrounded: by beautiful, kind faces.
They say they are from a Club, the Phillis Wheatley club in
Buffalo, New York—that they have something to give me. I've
worked so hard all my life, but now I have a place for people to
go, freed people, the sick, the vulnerable, the elderly: a white
wooden house, with a porch all around; and now, I need that
care. Who would have thought?

Me, in the John Brown Hall, infirmary, and main dormitory.
My parents are no longer with me, but I remember how we
would spend time, walking around my farm, seeing the birds,
the trees, The Sun, bright yet soft, like a butter yellow, and
it forms a skylight. My house, brick, thanks to my husband,
my love, who has flown skyward to that heavenly realm some
years before. Bless him. A house paid for with baked goods,
root beer, and the bounty from the garden: All a labour of
love: But I got it done. It's not a big house, but comfortable,
something comfortable. I am at peace there. I think about
my husband, I think about Nelson, but these women, from
Buffalo, New York, they are doing this for me. They are raising
money for me. Me. I don't know what to say. Blessed me.

I have no words, so they hugged me, and told me, with
the help of other clubs they have raised enough for me to
have a monthly pension. I had Nothing fighting three
decades for a military pension, $20.00 a month, but that's not
enough—I'm talking about survival, not just for me, but for
the people who stay at this place, what I wanted for them, and
now, I am here too, so, how God works. These women, I was

trying to create an existence, for myself and my parents, and others, all this time. Phillis, I have to thank you.

I have no words: poetess, intellectual, a woman who did right by her people. They told me abolitionist was in your blood, in your words, inspiring people like Edmund Quincy. Why am I not surprised? Us women, we get it done. Us black women we get it done. It's in the details: the Doin' . . . Yes, it's in the details. I might not be able to read or write, but I know Phillis that you were the first, to lead our people out of the wilderness to the Promised Land. It starts with one.

It only takes one. May God continue to bless you and all of your achievements. You were not alive to see all of our people free, but from up there, where you are, you know it to be true, and you are smiling, smiling, and rejoicing with all of the angels. The Civil War – I was a spy, I was a nurse, I did it all—for my people, and with your writing, what you had up in that head, you did it for us too. Your words: Silver    Drops      Of       Rain. Be at peace, dear One:  rest your head on a pillow of stars, a bed of stardust. Yes, Dear One, Rest, Rest, and be at peace.

# Lewis Adams: 1881

I loved to fashion things out of tin, make something new out
of the metal that emanated silver. Teapots, chandeliers, once
I made a lamp with parts that looked like wings: a silver bird
about to fly away. A tinsmith is an artisan, and I enjoyed
having the ability to put my artistic touches on household
things, things used in the everyday, that still could be pieces of
art. I was not able to go to art school, but I could be an artisan
as well as a tradesman, and that gave me great satisfaction and
a sense of peace. Thoughts were rising, moving, puffs of white
sailing through an aerial sea, atmospheric: pulsing   Pulsing
Thoughts are now descending, wisps of – they enter the portal
. . . "Booker, Booker T.," I said to myself, "he was a determined
young man."

General Samuel C. Armstrong, founder of the Hampton
Institute, told me so, he had a Fire—not unlike my hearth,
where I would twist and shape the tin into whatever desired
shape.

My people, the people of Tuskegee need a hand up, a step up...
not a handout. Would we get a chance? A road to Damascus:
$2,000 annually secured from the Alabama legislature, with
the help of two white Democrats, Colonel Wilbur F. Foster,
who was a Confederate soldier, and  Arthur L. Brooks, as well
as a former slave owner, now banker, George W. Campbell.
We now need a Wizard, and I think Booker T. is our man. I
taught myself French, Spanish, and German, with a will
forged in steel, a school of the highly motivated, which is what
our people need to be.

I think of Phillis. Another highly motivated soul. I know that Booker and I will be talking about her, discussing her poetry, how education was the golden-lit tunnel that led to her freedom. Learning English, Greek, and Latin, it was the thread that pulled everything together, creating a quilt that kept her aspirations warm, aspirations for her freedom.

The school is going to be a shack, not much, but I see so much potential. I will introduce this Booker T. to members of our community, so they can see, so He Can See. Hope is a Spring that can become a river, that can course into an ocean . . . Yes. Booker T.

A community entering transition. A community transformed: Rising from the ashes, becoming a Force. This is what I see. God, help us in this endeavour. May the Angels guide our way. We cannot give up, we are so close to something, I can taste it. The feeling of Metamorphosis in the Air. It has to get started somewhere, and it might as well be here. Tuskegee, Booker, me, all our people in this town— Change Is Calling.

# Booker: 1896

Phillis, Inspiration, Ancestor, I am willing this institution
into existence ... The Tuskegee Institute, teaching, giving
those practical skills to give Ourselves a future ... but your
words, your guidance still shapes me.    To   Traverse those
Boundaries that    should    only    be    in    the mind. This
gives us Hope. Yes, Phillis. And another one is coming on
Board.

Fall. The leaves.   Swirling ... Swirling ... The   Pippin   The
Roses    Somehow, I feel. The Call. The Call.  Something
Is About to CHANGE. I Sense    W H I S P E R S    It— The
burning orange, the fiery reds, The rustic brown, Something is
about to shift, twist, and shape into something: SOMETHING.

George Washington Carver.  A bright mind. A compassionate
soul. He'll help our people. He'll help to lead. He says the
peanut is the key. Alternatives to the cotton crop. Who knew?
He seems a little unorthodox, wanting to walk in nature in
his spare time, easel in hand, and paint trees, but I think it'll
be all right. I think it'll be fine, I think it will work. He has a
fire. A curiosity that will inspire my students. Yes, Phillis, I
think he is the one who will help us to progress. His mother,
he didn't know — kidnapped   by   slavers   His brother:
Some   Remnants    A bible, his only memory of her: the only
keepsake. It's memories, in old books, libraries, yes, in so
many things. Yes, Yes, It Is Home.

Phillis:

Halcyon Of—


Gourd:   Echoes   of   Sound


Pinwheels

      Pushing

           Through


     A                 STEP


      In

       The

        Sand


     Halcyon—


Burst of     The Planets     The embers of The Stars:  Dust:
Twinkle    Trails Of—

  What's   mentioned in

This Catalogue: The   Nebulae   Charted
By Charles Messier

The Celestial,   Star   Making:      Galaxies   Of   Light
And   Sound:  Silence


Map Making

The Universe      What Could
Be   What can Be


The Mystical Depths     The Mystical
Trains Of Thought


I think about Harvard:  Phillis'   Cambridge Of New-England
What I could Grasp:  Not Wisps of air   But Concrete,    Made
Real: Honorary Master's Degree.    I     Remember    I   Don't
Forget

The   Wisps   of   air    that surround me,   but   no
Vacuum    No vacuum of The Mind, Of The Spirit, The
OtherWorld always awaits. Our Ancestors always knew. They
Always

 They Walk Among Us, And They Say: "The Battle still
continues, and with our words, our minds as armour, We'll
win the fight, but the victories, like the defeats will be in
waves. Yes, they'll be in waves."

  We have to be ready   To   Swim    We Have To Be
READY

  Heaven:  The Cosmic Ocean   The   Realm   That

Looks

      Over

            Us      Lagoons      Of    Light

                You are a part of that

Phillis.

        You are a part of this.         A piece of

us. A Piece Of This.


              God bless you.        God

Bless us.

      Phillis, I will be At The Ready, as will you—as

you always were.

# Orion: 1921

### Marcus Garvey

We moved through water, through Time and Space, Space and Time: The Black Star Line, a fleet of ships sailing to The West Indies, Latin America; Reaching Jamaica, Cuba, Panama, Costa Rica. Remembering Our Homeland and  Liberia  A ghost-like dream—Africa: She spoke to us, like Phillis did, and the spirit guided us, Like The Poetess From Senegambia.

Her star, our star, she talked about it in her poems, the North Star, an Unfettered Celestial Focus, Phillis, her poetry:  it was the beacon still  leading  us  all  inspiring activists like Edmund Quincy,  yes, white, but helped us in our cause, for we need all nations, all people to help us, An  Army Yes

　　　　　An   Army.

Liberia, will it be a failure? The Black Star Line:  Giving our people a chance, to start over

　　somewhere　　else　　I　　don't　　know.　I feel trepidatious　　From Jamaica, to here, to where, so many people depending on me: Marcus Garvey, leader of the Universal Negro Improvement Association. The Engine To— Will I make the right decision? I just don't know.

I just don't—

I hear the Ancestors, the same ones who called on Phillis, to write those words, to guide her on the Path—a Springboard to thought made concrete, forged in sight and sound.  Through the linguistic, the Spirits guided her home.  Guided her home.

Yes, yes. Yes. Phillis, I call on you now to show me, guide me.
I don't know quite where this will lead. Will there be danger,
failure, regret? But to stay here? Where they Just—

   This dream of mine, The Black Star Line, the exodus
to Liberia, will it fall apart, a building crumbling to its
foundations . . . ? A floating triptych, a marine vessel, the
Orion, now proclaims  your name, Phillis, a shepherdess
leading her flock. The echoes of footsteps sonorous in     an
abandoned    hallway. You . . .


How can we . . . ? To Resurface. How can we . . . ?
Metamorphosis. How can we . . . ?

Quagmires scar     the     Landscape     The Brass Ring   What
is Possible For my People?

Water As Mirror, Water As Beacon, Water as Mourning Gaps
of Air Cutting Into A Surge of—

The Waves     an aquatic Tower     the Drawbridge,     Our
BLOOD     We Try to Forget,  But

Phillis: We must bring our people home—To be Loved. To Be
Cherished, and to be At Peace. This is all I ask.

Phillis, you have endured so much for so long. You, how could
you bear it, to have such gifts, but to be denied:  no talking
circuits, no more books to be published, yet   the ink of our
stories running through     your     veins   Years later, you
waited for your time, but it wasn't easy, it wasn't meant to be—
dying alone, another child at your breast; Before, a daughter
who pushed out her last breath, you watching your other child
die. Hard, everything                 so     hard   Scullery maid:
Not teaching, Not learning. Not able to inspire others while

being paid a salary to exude gifts which would help future generations.

Phillis, the Zenith, the North Star, a Constellation, your life is written in the stars, and there will be those who will follow after you. It will be all right. I pray for it to be all right. Liberia: I pray that it will be successful . . . and that you, Phillis, will Continue To Shine Down on us With Your Love.

# Mildred Massey

1957

Sparkling green eyes, fair skin, they called me coloured, negro
. . . skin as light as theirs . . . but we Kept   Going   there was
so much I wanted to do; so much that I wanted to accomplish,
my dad was the first person of colour to be a letter carrier in
El Paso. Fluent Spanish flowed from his tongue, and he was a
graduate from Houston-Tillotson College in Texas.

My father  handsome   glowing mocha skin  emulating his
Native American and black roots. My mother: the soft surge of
life that gave us no choice, but to keep going; It would always
be—Me, a Student    an all black school: Douglass Elementary
and High School.   Scholarship: swimming through an
educational stream—liberal arts at Houston-Tillotson College.
Then, More practical:  a transfer to Southern University in
Baton Rouge   the Business        Administration      Program;
Not Enough, NO:  woman of colour,  Summer School at Prairie
View College in Texas.

Reward, the Holy Grail:  registrar and secretary to the
President   Norfolk division of  Now, Norfolk State
University. Homecoming: El Paso, Mother, to my girls,
Later, while working, Attending what is now the University
Of Texas, in El Paso; I  became part of   The   Force that is
desegregation in that school. All   of   these   things   These
Experiences These   memories   would lead me to where I
am today

And my girl, the oldest,    Barbara    how she came into the
world: Dragged along the birth canal with forceps because
they wouldn't give me a caesarean, but she   has    spunk.
There is something—

I will keep going for her, and all my girls. This life is not easy.
But I will keep going, And Phillis: There's a club, the Phillis
Wheatley Club, one that helps young women like myself get a
situation, a start in life: one foot in front of the other.

All I need is a hand up, not a handout, a step up. I'm now
a member, and part of the workforce, here in El Paso, my
employer, the USO. Later, I would be the first woman of colour
to be a clerical worker at Fort Bliss in the Postal Locator.

# The First

The first to be a clerical worker at Fort Bliss, the first to work at the Veterans Administration Hospital in Sylmar, California the   first   to  I had to keep going, not so much because I wanted to be the trailblazer, it was just something that had to be done, to raise my family, to raise my girls, to give them a start. A  Start  In  Life   A  start  That is what I had to do: that's   what—

# *She Looks~*

"She looks like a Mexican."   fluid like water they don't
understand how we can come from different worlds
sometimes  the  genesis  was  a  cage, sexual  exploitation
other times it was just love . . . these  things  did  happen  so
much  to  explain, but there are people who want to put us
in a box, but it's Not so easy. For those of us, skin as light as
theirs . . .            They   don't   know   what   to   do

 But I remember my history, the sadness, the scars, but there
were also moments of joy . . . they can't take that     away
from   us, and I will teach all my daughters:

                    Do   not

let     them     take    away

your     joy.

# Step: 1973

BARBARA LEE

Steeped, I'm stepping into the waves, green, they form a quadrangle, the oval lawn and Holmgren Meadows, Mills College, California, transformation . . . But I remember, the glow of blue, green, yellow, the fireflies in the San Fernando Valley, framed by the Santa Monica Mountains. I walk down between the Corinthian columns, Mills Hall. Memories rush in . . .

My mother was a member of the Phillis Wheatley club, a staircase to entering a sisterhood of connections, social, business: A Bridge An organization that also helped women migrating from the South to the North, After Emancipation: A New Life. My mother, Mildred Massey, worked for the USO; she also attended Texas Western College, which later became University Of Texas in El Paso. My mom on the forefront, education: it was the key, she told me about Phillis, child prodigy, easily learning English, Latin, Greek, and so on. Creating her own opportunity so she could be free . . . the book was the genesis. The first, she was the first black American to publish a book of poetry—and she was a Slave.

Water is rushing in, and the wave the breath of the wind on the grass, it's an ocean of green, the air, the Zephyr's breath riding the waves: Phillis, you were the key, Phillis, you are the key, education as cinder, a staircase, a hallowed hallway leading to somewhere; A voyage on the seas of knowledge, travelling different worlds with The Word as our compass. You See, We See. My mom was able to work full time, because of that Voyage, and being a member of a circle started by you. By YOU. Yes, YOU. I thank you. My mother thanks you.

We remember what you sacrificed, what you gave, instead of remaining in England, a country who recognized and appreciated your gifts, you went back to America out of a sense of obligation, your sick mistress . . . Who did believe in you, but didn't keep you safe from what you were, a slave, not receiving any financial freedom from a will, but forced, imprisoned into a life of poverty and never-ending hardship. Phillis, you did what you could. You did what you thought was right. We remember by honouring you, and moving forward, the best way we can. Your dreams were written in the stars, and we follow them, like those who followed the North Star to freedom. We don't forget. We never will.

# A Path: Barbara Lee 2019

I remember, Phillis, as I became State Senator of the California
State Assembly . . .

A Momentous Day in 1996: I know you were
Smiling    Down    On    Me

My mother, Mildred Massey, Emanated A Glow Of Pride

And now, I am speaking about the AIDS Memorial Quilt:
November, 2019, A remembrance to those who passed away,
entering the ethereal realm because of a disease that incited
ignorance, prejudice, about sexual orientation, stereotypes . . .
Alarm, panic in the 80's The homage to books, the lair
literary, it was a perfect space to talk about remembering, the
power of Story, those we had lost.

The Great Hall, in the Library Of Congress, with angels
looking down over me, and colonnades sculpted with the
greatest finery: the colours, orange, red, green. I   Remember.
And the circle, the desks of oak, the figures, the patronesses
of Art, Poetry, Philosophy, the disciplines that shape and
cultivate humanity. The talk was meant to be here, I was
meant to be here, Congresswoman, one who sees injustice, but
through the proponents of Story, to hear people's voices, there
can be   A   Shift. We cannot lose our moral compass. Society
needs an anchor: us, to stand up for each other. That is what is
needed.

And so I am here, in the Library Of Congress, to talk about
a project that will archive important stories about a struggle,

a crisis from the past. Yes. And as I remember the circle of oak desks, in the Reading Room, the jewel of the Jefferson building, and that beloved dome, proclaiming all civilizations to have value, I smile. I am here at last. A young girl from El Paso, a young black girl from El Paso, with a scar from a cut above her eye, from a delivery with complications . . . because my mother was a woman of colour . . . I don't forget. But I am here. I am here, and I feel at peace.

## Universe: 2020


Me, now Congresswoman:
22 Years—
Still Serving     The     PEOPLE:

Ascending The Stars
Nebula
Flashing


Shimmering


Lost


But—


Trying


Star

Shining Bright:

Burning Out

Trying to Find

You                                    Grasped


                              Ember



                You were the Spark




                                Flame

You created

Music

Constellation

You were a Guide

Didn't Mislead

Orion

You left a mark



Comet



You were a Litany Of Light



You didn't give up

A   River


Star Dust


Sprinkling Your Magic And Your—

With "Thoughts On The Works Of Providence,"

You Reminded Us That We Were Philosophers,
Scientists, Astronomers,

Charting Stars, Planets, The Cosmos

We Were Scientists, Mathematicians,

You told us so we wouldn't forget

You Told Us

You Told Us

You—

## 2020
# The Future—Part II: The Chorus

B

bright

star

love          loss

did we do enough?

did we do too little?

the fight

the battle

we must

you must

fire

light

star

bright

rays

brilliance

not hidden

embraced

our goal

our prayer

you kept going

so will I

so will We

trudging

plodding forward

yes

                              you



                    i


                         remember

i


        believe




                         hope




        embrace—

yes

didn't              give up

they say

i try

sometimes discouraged

academia

being At The Table

no—

        they don't accept us


      we create

           our own

                    bastions

         of knowledge


a way around the system


we    teach



        artists   students   teachers
tradespeople:



              we    know



Reverberations   Dr.    King     Resurrection City  June
1968  Solidarity Day

           A United Force

      we    believe

you  phillis

should have been

teaching at the apex

    oxford      cambridge

        harvard: the cambridge
of New-England

   only in your mind,

     the nation of equal opportunity:

    imagination,

  and in the realm of your poetry,

 that mystical state,

    or country within a country.

phillis

a     call

phillis

a

meditation

phillis

a     song

phillis

a     thought

phillis
a   pause

but your name

always synonymous


with possibility,

hope,

and tenacious

in the face of adversity        a baptism by fire

a stand,

a stance,

in grace,

self respect and confidence,

surrounded by humility.

## Cosmos

beginning

journey

doubt

hope

trepidation

love

friendship

darkness

light

dark

you

me

angels

home

books

the word

portals

a lifeline

a guideline

a heeding

a warning

following

the path

and

opening up

yourself

to the unknown.

# M

moon light

moon Drop

going      floating

rivers of stars: phillis

i read your words: a light   a    light

do

we?

should we?

you see

yes


yes


yes


sometimes, things are uncertain: black star,


north star


emancipation


floating sails of ivory


reams of cloud:  they don't REVEAL the      nightmares

ghost-like, sometimes settling at the bottom of

the

DEPTHS


the skeleton of lies, the phantoms of
exploitation   the Death,

the Death:

bodies, THE—tombs of sadness, tombs of
dead    dreams

corpses:   mummified, like our visions
but we rise AGAIN,

and the voices whisper . . .



phillis,



i remember,



the ancestral memory.



yes,

they speak

in bright colours: fuchsia, red, indigo . . .

they speak out loud,

in colour, our dreams pathways

highways

phillis, i have been to oxford, will go to cambridge, i see with
your eyes,

your imagination was always a bridge . . .

a

bridge

a—

the circular, the circular . . .

yes, you should have been, but WE keep fighting for

we keep fighting for—

the silver lining.

we aerate light and purpose

we

we

we

we forge On:

a choir, a symphony,


yes, and you oh, you,

the angels see past the precipice: they saw, they have seen, they
know


oh phillis, yes, they have seen. oh  phillis—and the ancestors—


with every step, more progress, they have seen, will see


so we keep soldiering on, we keep soldiering ON . . .


an army of light,


we must keep moving forward. yes, phillis, yes, phillis,


We cannot give Up, Holding on to Possibility.

# PART III

## Iter Sustinet

# Remembering—Part I

I am on a ship, like the London Packet, the moon, Diana, is
at my side, and Venus, like on the voyage to Britannia as my
Earthly self . . . I am reflecting, memories upon memory, like
a foundation of thoughts words and images, a pyramid of
meditation. It is coming, waves   of   Waves The pathways
of my brain are on Fire, Lit Up,  A   Surge  Yes, Yes, And they
Say, and I Remember, going, shifting Back in Time. Before my
words became wings and were made concrete in September
1773, a book that was   a   key  A book that was   The   Key

# Phoebe

Shining

Your strength,

    your support,

        surrounds me, envelopes me like a silver
cloud.

    These memories are manifesting ink,

      a marriage of solid and liquid and squid.

        I thank you, Phoebe, goddess
of the Moon,

and all your Sisters,

      Mother Mnemosyne, her daughters,

     And my Mama, who are part of this
sacred circle:

one with no beginning, and no end, as the past, present, and
future converge.

      Words are my sanctuary,

     where I can rest my weary head,

    up-ended by stars, suspended in the violet sky.

The choir of the cosmos is twinkling spirituals of white light.

As I sift through these pages, touched by dreams,

My Eyes . . .

None Of This Would Have Been Possible Without—

And The Ancestors . . .

You are a part of this Creative Core. I sit back, and nod.

This was meant to be. The Time is Coming.

Soon, we will all be Free:

The Shackles, Cast Off,   D e s t r o y e d

Phoebe, Monarch Of The Moon, you called to me,

I had to channel you,

even though I was referring to your brother, Pheobus, the Sun King, but I had to include you . . .

"The Train of Stars," the signposts for my people.

Those courageous enough to flee North,

to this Promised Land, that I cannot be a party to. No.

I made a call, beseeched Maecenas,

navigating the two worlds,

invoking two meanings, patron:
conduit to freedom,

as well as supporter of the arts. Double
wordplay my two-edged sword,

and The Battle goes underground, so that I
can make my plea.

Referring to the pastoral, the river synonymous
with freedom,

the banks of which Sharp was walking along,

and other compatriots, assisting
Those in Need.

Parnassus, a mystical enclave, a poetic embrace, asking for
Maecenas' blessing,

this is my Zephyr, so I can continue to
sing out.

My notes: vowels and consonants, playing
the 26 keys,

so I can create my song.

The sable Israelites are following that Star
on the horizon.

I was able to follow you,

Phoebe, as well as your brother
Phoebus,

but it is you, Phoebe,

and your sister Aurora,

Queen Of The Dawn,

that nurtures the creativity

In Me,

        as I have invoked in my poetry, that tribute to
you, all of you,

              including Mother Mnemosyne,
and my own mother.

        I will never forget. Without you—


             Without . . .


        It won't be long now,


        I might not see it in this lifetime,


           the eradication of this moral disease:
the nightmare,


                shackled


                    and chained

I might be in the heavens, riding on that
"heavenly train" . . .

but that doesn't matter. Here it is. You. Me.

The Word that has
captivated and saved So Many Of Us.

And it all started with: that
papyrical lair,

that we could always run to, that circular
staircase;

it always leads to somewhere, never
feeling lost.

As I have felt, in Mather Byle's library, a
sense,
I had never experienced before,
comfort flying to me in volumes, letters,
and bookcases,
and when James Albert Ukasaw
Gronniosaw,

my brother, forged from kinship with

The Word, when he was on that ship, that Book.

That Book with a cross, it anchored him, prevented him,

from the madness that overtook many of us.

That Bible, He was able to   Hang On.

And because of The Word, those angels of paper, I am able to subsist.

It's A life, Not Easy, as one cannot go by appearance.

I am a puppet, with invisible strings.

I thank you all, The Mystical Sisters And Daughters.

And My Mother . . .

Ancestors, you have kept

Me sane.


Mama always said lean on them.


Remember. And when the seas get rough, You MUST hold on. You.

It will be All Right. You will make it.

You will Push THROUGH.

You Will.

Because the Ancestors had a purpose for you,

so You must plod on.

You have No Choice, even though it
is Hard.


It will be The HARDEST Thing You
DO.

I see that now.  I am at peace, and as I look out the window,
Phoebe, I don't feel so alone.

## Movement

Maybe, I'll write her—
This Countess Of Huntingdon . . .

I have a feeling that is what I should do:
Contact her,
Be in Communication;
I was thinking of
writing a poem about her chaplain . . .
Whitefield.

He just died, transfigured:  The Ethereal.
I would like to send my condolences:
Another soul that was held in high regard by many:
It is time to give pause, to pay tribute,
And I can

with

My
Words.
I will reach out to
this Lady Huntingdon.
The Mistress Susannah was also troubled by the passing of
this chaplain.
I will think about what to say, and have my pen and paper
ready.

I also think of James Albert Ukawsaw Gronniosaw,
Another writer, I esteem, who had this Lady Huntingdon as
his patron.

I enjoy and respect his work.
Telling the story of our people,
The struggles, not hushed in secret,
Like whispers in a hallway,
But screaming out for paper, hungering to be Illuminated by his Pen.
Why this came into my mind, I don't know.
What is the connection?
I see the ancestors in my mind's eye.
I don't know the answer, but I mull things over.
Gronniosaw writes about his experience being a slave, captive, escaping slavery,
And living in a place known for the abolitionists:
Those who advocate for our freedom.
I think of Granville Sharp who fought to keep a man from being re-enslaved.
And he won.
England.
Why do I get the feeling that it will play an important role in my future?
I will lie down.
Then, I will pay tribute to this chaplain, Whitefield,
Another elegy, for this writer,
As it is my duty to give homage to those who have passed from this life,
And enter the next. I feel it is an honour. And a duty. So I must.
But first, I must rest.

# Remembering—Part II

My Celestial Self, continuing to Time Travel back into The Past, the year of my death, 1784, remembering Obour, our connection, kismet, Sisters in Spirit . . . Wherever I go, she is with me, so I see her, even now, and from time to time revisit the terrestrial plane. And so I do again, to see her again, now that I am Siptoraaki. I can almost touch her. Obour, I miss so much . . .

# Thinking Of You: 1784

Death  Shroud  The Sickle  The Circle  Birth  Death  Life:
Seasons, they Change

Son  Buried  with  Mother  His terminated breath:  drawn
exhaled  cold room Three Hours Later

Friend: Your exodus is complete  You are the Moses  Your
words  A light Torched by Liquid

A papyric chain  That will START  I see a young man  inspired
by your words  A Catalyst That will Spark Him  To Get ALL
Our People FREE

Me, Obour, your Sister, And     I     am     remembering

Reading your letters . . . over and over . . . My Dear Obour . . .
My Dear Obour—


The Israelites of SABLE  keep marching, Obstacles—But
Renewal Inevitable:

Their eyes,  Lamps, For they SEE  A Road Emblazoned:
opportunity  a path with twists

and forks  It all  Started with YOU  My Friend  Susannah The
Mistress  The yoke

that pulled you BACK  You felt guilty  Indebted  Your
Conscience  Another Currency  Arrears

fulfill an obligation Your Book THE PRICE for in the land
where the Stronghold was

Somerset you would have roamed free and prospered: Your
subjects Phonetic Chromatic


A Chorus Of 26 chords A symphony of FINERY Lays Those
Songs Being Sung Music

Played The Synergy of Black and White That Will Elude Us
In This Lifetime

But might come in the NEXT You Suffered haunted riddled
with NIGHTMARES

about how we were taken And That Wooden Beast that had
swallowed us whole:

"*The Phillis . . .* " So Many Ghosts, and yet You—The
Ancestors They will Never Forsake Us

Memories Continue To Resurface—That Demon Of Oak
Spitting Us Out Onto A Friendless, Alien Shore—

My friend I love you, and I'm proud to call you friend You
and I are part of a chain, momentum that cannot stop now.

God, Jesus are smiling now The Ancestors Jubilant They
Rejoice You will take us to

the Promised Land With Your Words With Your Song I will
miss you, Friend

Dear One, but I will look for you in the heavens skyward:
Racing across the sky

With Mother Mnemosyne,  Her Daughters,  Her Sisters,
Aurora, Phoebe

Your Love In The Stars  another signpost for Our People:  An
Orb Of Light And Colour

An Aerial Flame  You are  the Maecenas  The Ovid  The
Homer  May you take Refuge In The Stars.

# Remembering—Part III

The wheels spin faster, faster, like a maelstrom. I am feeling,
sinking into feeling, it's an ocean,  a storm rushing, the
waves are screeching, screech, like birds in mourning, I am
remembering what happened . . . The last day of breath . . . in
December, 1784 . . .  It    was    so    cold    I am remembering
being submerged, then silence, then, a lack of light, then
a silence, a strange music, I think I saw pinpricks of light,
pinpricks. Moving like a pinwheel, faster and faster, the
streams of light becoming stronger and stronger, and my body
it was as if I was   flailing     flailing  I was scared, but  At  The
Same   Time  The Ancestors they were calling to me louder
and louder they said They   Said:


S    O    O    N

# Dream

Flashes of light
Surround it . . .
Ink of colour—
A bright black—
From the iron gall
My work.
Dream.
A dream
That manifested.
Demanding our FREEDOM.
Words, the messengers:
Ideas flying into people's minds
Doves going Skyward
But now,
Scullery maid,
I consort with
Floors now,
Wash walls,
Carry basins:
Working for a boarding house
Publishing more books,
Teaching,
Not a possibility:
I am denied,
Because of the ink of my skin.
We are not accepted.
The Army cannot cross the moat,
And invade the stronghold.
My creativity,

Stifled,
But not
STRANGLED
And, without the opportunities,
What is the use of an education?
Yes, I am grateful for what I have
Been GIVEN
But, that's not Enough—
I wanted to do more:
Fill the depths
With knowledge,
The students willing vessels;
My words an eagerly awaited compendium
Contributing to society
With my gifts
My skills netting a livelihood
Not flour
Going through the sieve
But NOW . . .
No patrons
The Revolutionary War
Those with England
Stay at their peril
Beaten up, threatened,
The cloud of interrogation, fear,
Mistrust hangs heavily in the air,
Cooperation has evaporated
There is no one to help me now:
No one to buy my books
No one to offer me a place to live
No one able to offer me a decent job,
Even if it is domestic:
Maid, or a cook
The vestiges of support are destroyed
Community disintegrated

I am all alone.
Husband in jail
Debt is the crime
No money,
A sin
My children, Death took them away from me
They are with the Angels now,
For their lives were snuffed out.
He—
His life,
Now, the only one . . .
A bud slowly opening in spring
He rests on my chest
Mother,
And Mother Mnemosyne
Give me the strength,
The courage,
To dream my way out of this one—
Two children,
The murderer, poverty . . .
Starvation:
The death sentence
What could have been
Should have been
My finest creation . . .
I see them now:
The Ancestors in a procession, the robes flowing in the wind,
The walking sticks, the headdresses of glowing colour,
The gold and emerald
Faces shining with pride,
Love in the eyes,
Mirth, joy, in the high cheekbones,
Blue highlights in the jet black hair
I see someone familiar,
She is enshrouded in black, but her face is hidden,

They are walking along the shore, verdant, teeming with palm
trees
Singing a sweetness that I have never heard before
Yes.
They are motioning to me now.
They are calling to me.
Soon, it will be time.
The ones in front are jumping into song and dance,
The drum a familiar rhythm, a comforting heartbeat
I am ready for the call.

But until then,
There is the dreaming.

# Afterword

Thinking about Phillis, three words come to mind: bravery, perseverance, and hope. A scared young girl of eight, coming to a strange new world in 1761, never to see her parents ever again—that's a hard thing for people to imagine. There on that new shore was John Wheatley, a successful tailor and merchant, looking for a companion for his wife, Susannah—probably to replace the loss of their daughter, Sarah, who died some years before.[1]

Did Phillis ever think she would make history—herstory? To have to deal with the demons—and possible sexual assault—on the slave ship the *Phillis*, where she ironically got her name . . . how did she have the courage to trust, and move forward? She knew she had to survive, but how? For her to learn English, Latin, and Greek—languages not of her native tongue, and at such a young age—that would not have been easy. For her to know that her propensity for language, for writing, would be the gateway to freedom, but that she would have to learn her craft or get help from people who were slave owners or proponents of slavery—that would not be easy, and shows courage on this journey.[2]

Phillis published her first poem at fourteen years of age, and it appeared in *The Newport Mercury* in December 1767.[3] As a person of colour, she must have felt that she had a duty to advocate for her people through her literary art, and bring readers to her cause.

One such prominent person was Edmund Quincy (1808–1877), whose grandmother had a copy of Phillis' poetry.[4] Quincy was the second son of Josiah Quincy III, a graduate and later president of Harvard University. Like his father, Edmund also graduated from Harvard, where he trained as a lawyer. Despite his privileged background, his path changed to one of advocating for the end of slavery. Quincy was inspired to become an abolitionist not only by Phillis' poetry, but also by the murder of Elijah Lovejoy. Lovejoy died at the hands of a pro-slavery mob in Illinois on November 7, 1837 while defending the site of his anti-slavery newspaper, *The Saint Louis Observer*.[5] Quincy would go on to work with many abolitionists, and became the editor of the *Non-Resistant*, an official paper for the abolitionist movement. He was also guest editor of *The Liberator*, a newspaper published by William Lloyd Garrison, another well-known abolitionist.

Phillis lit a candle to many, another victory of her legacy. To work on those poems at night, and in the early morning, when she had peace, where she could open herself up to the creative, think about her mother, father, and the life that she had led, and write these experiences into her poems—that was a victory, and shows perseverance. Margaretta Matilda Odell, great grandniece of Susannah Wheatley, wrote in her biography about Phillis, that she remembered, " . . . that her mother poured out water before the sun at his rising."[6] This was a Fulani custom, and that is what Phillis' mother did. Her past life was not forgotten.

Phillis knew that publishing her work would lead to her freedom. Securing a patron, Selina Hastings, the Countess of Huntingdon, thanks to her mistress, was another victory. Phillis wrote a poem, "On the death of the Rev. Mr. George Whitefield. 1770.," a dedication, an elegy to George Whitefield, the Countess' chaplain. Somehow, she knew it would be a bridge to Lady Huntingdon being her patron, and subsequent publication. This poem, about the Countess' chaplain George Whitefield, a British Reverend, a slave owner, and one of the founders of the Methodist denomination who made numerous trips to America to proselytize, changed Phillis' life forever.[7] As written by Vincent Carretta, "Wheatley's elegy on Whitefield brought her almost instant intercolonial and transatlantic fame after it appeared on October 11, 1770."[8]

The Countess of Huntingdon was a major advocate for Black people who wanted to join the Christian ministry, and also guided those on the pathway of publication such as James Albert Gronniosaw Ukasaw and Olaudah Equiano. Ironically she herself became a slave owner, when she inherited Whitefield's slaves in Georgia upon his death in 1770, but her Christian convictions led her to believe that she should assist all those who wanted to spread the word of God through ministry.[9] It was through the Countess' efforts that an African American, John Marrant, became "the first formally ordained Black preacher in North America."[10] The Countess of Huntingdon embodied many contradictions, but she did help create a, " . . . tradition of English speaking writers of African descent . . . [by] enabling such writers to gain access to print."[11]

As I mentioned previously, the Countess' chaplain formed the subject of Phillis' inspiring poem "On the Death of the Rev. George Whitefield. 1770." Whitefield's talks drew large crowds—for instance, when his tour took him to Philadelphia in 1739, approximately 8,000 people showed up to hear his words.[12] What is significant about her poem is how through the voice of Whitefield Phillis subverts Whitefield's views of slavery and, ". . . addresses his message of salvation through Christ through two separate audiences: 'my dear Americans' and 'ye Africans.' Prominently identified in the poem's headnote as being of African descent, 'by Phillis, a Servant Girl of 17 years of age . . . And has been but 9 years in this Country from Africa,' Wheatley's consistent use of the first-person plural *we* renders people of both European and African descent equally American."[13] In Phillis eyes, through salvation from Christ, everyone can be an equal part of a community.[14] By being Christian, everyone can belong, be they Black or white. Phillis' poem proposes that religion—having Christian beliefs—can be a unifying force.

Another significant aspect of this poem is how Phillis addresses the Countess Huntingdon directly, venerating and praising her. Phillis writes:

> Great Countess! We *Americans* revere
> Thy name, and thus condole thy grief sincere:
> We mourn with thee, that Tomb obscurely plac'd,
> In which thy Chaplain undisturb'd rest.[15]

Phillis knew about the Countess because she was part of her mistress' social network, and she had heard of George Whitefield and his charismatic sermons because he came to North America on talking tours seven times.[16] She may have even heard Whitefield speak when he was in Boston before he died. [17] I think she knew that the Countess would help her on the journey to publication, and in this poem she cleverly appeals to the Countess' sentiments. Phillis astutely honours Whitefield while at the same time undermining Whitefield's pro-slavery stance and uplifting the Countess' more supportive views of Black liberation, embodying the Countess' contradictions while still advancing a message of equality of Black people. That shows intuition and intelligence.

Phillis' writing, her relationship with the Countess of Huntingdon, and the publication of her book would ultimately lead her to England to promote her book in 1773. It must have been strange for her to visit this country. Just a year before in 1772 the Somerset case, *Somerset v Stewart*, had set the precedent that any slave who reached England's shores had the opportunity to gain their freedom. Though Phillis does not seem to have used this legal precedent to assert her freedom upon her arrival in England, she likely felt this trip would be helpful in her quest to seek her liberation. Indeed, during her trip she met a significant abolitionist figure in England—Granville Sharp—who had played a role in the Somerset case.[18]

Sharp was the son of the Archbishop of Northumberland. The family had many children and couldn't afford an advanced education for all of them, so Sharp apprenticed as a linen draper, ultimately finding a position as a civil servant.[19] His interests turned to social justice when a slave from Barbados, Jonathan Strong, sought help from Sharp's brother, Jonathan Sharp, a doctor, "who treated the poor of the City of London for free."[20] Strong had been pistol whipped by his Master, the lawyer David Lisle. Gravely injured, the Sharp brothers helped Strong receive medical treatment, and upon his recovery found him a job. Lisle ultimately discovered Strong and without capturing him sold him to another—a Jamaica planter named James Kerr. It was arranged for him to be taken by ship away from England to Jamaica. Two slave catchers hired by Lisle captured Strong and put him in jail. When Sharp was told, he intervened, and with the help of the Lord Mayor of London, Strong was set free. However, Sharp was then informed that Strong was still legally a slave, and the planter's property. Sharp, not to be deterred, bought a whole law library, fought the case, and the two plaintiffs were so intimidated by Sharp's legal defense that they dropped their charges, and Strong remained free. Unfortunately, this case did not set any legal precedents, but that opportunity would soon arrive with the Somerset case.[21]

James Somerset was a slave bought by Charles Stewart, a high-ranking colonial customs official, in Virginia on August 1, 1749. Somerset went to England with Charles Stewart in November 1769, and ran away in October 1771. Stewart captured Somerset on November 26, intending to send him to Jamaica on a ship under the command of Captain John Knowles.

The British African community got word of these events and plans to Granville Sharp, and he, along with some others, immediately submitted a request to a Judge Mansfield to issue a writ of habeas corpus ordering the captain to bring Somerset before the court. Sharp successfully convinced several people to take on the case free of charge, including lawyer Francis Hargrave, who wrote an unforgettable account of his experience arguing the case, and went on to a successful legal career.

Mansfield unsuccessfully attempted to get the two parties to settle out of court, so he was forced to render a decision. It would be a decision that would have an unforgettable impact on so many lives, including Phillis Wheatley's.[22] The decision? Mansfield "ruled that an owner could not legally force a slave in England back to the colonies." As Carretta reflects, " . . . the judgment was widely considered then and since as the moment slavery was abolished in England."[23] Phillis knew that by going to England to promote her book, and meeting abolitionists like Sharp, that she was taking steps towards her freedom. Indeed, Phillis writes as much in a letter to David Wooster. In her letter she surmises that the publication of *Poems On Various Subjects* and the support of the British abolitionists helped her secure her freedom, as she was manumitted as soon as she returned to America after her trip to England.[24]

Wooster himself was a significant figure, and he and his family were of great importance in Phillis' life. He and his family supported Phillis, promoting her book to their friends and selling copies. A general in the Revolutionary War, Wooster was fatally injured in battle and died on May 2, 1777.[25]

Phillis wrote an elegy for Wooster, which she sent to his family along with a letter offering her condolences to Wooster's widow Mary, and reflecting on the support both she and her late husband had offered to the poet. As Mukhtar Ali Isani notes, " 'On the Death of General Wooster' is [not] only an elegy composed to comfort the general's wife, but also an expression of the gratitude for the interest of the Woosters in Wheatley's fortunes and in the welfare of African slaves in general," quoting the following from Wheatley's poem:

> But how, presumptuous shall we hope to find
> Divine acceptance with the Almighty mind,
> While yet (O deed Ungenerous!) they disgrace
> And hold in bondage Afric's blameless race? [26]

Here Phillis highlights the cruel irony that many Americans fighting for their freedom and independence from England did not think it was necessary to free slaves in America, an opinion not shared by the compassionate Wooster.[27]

Phillis then writes, "You will do me a great favour by returning to me by the first oppy those books that remain unsold and remitting the money for those that are sold . . . I am greatly obliged to you for the care you show me, and your condescention in taking so much pains for my Interest . . . "[28]

Phillis had found many allies in her lifetime through her work. Unfortunately, many of those allies like Wooster had either died in the war, fighting on the Revolutionary side, or had left the country for England, because of the rising anger and resentment toward those who remained loyal to England.

One of her supporters, who had signed the attestation acknowledging that she was the author of the poems, was Thomas Hutchinson, Governor of Massachusetts Bay. Being the Royal Governor, he faced anger and resentment because of his association with England. Hutchinson left America for England in 1774, remaining in exile there until his death. Even though he was against legislation like the Stamp Act, which "[taxed] virtually any document in the colonies, as well as on every newspaper and pamphlet published in the colonies, and even 'on every pack of playing cards, and all dice, which shall be sold or used within the said colonies and plantations'," a mob came to his house, and, " . . . broke the windows, smashed the furniture . . . scattered the library in the mud, broke down the doors and partitions, and were beginning to remove the roof when the dawn put an end to their systematic fury."[29] Even though the Stamp Act was repealed in 1766 by King George III because of mass opposition to it, the American colonists remained unhappy, with these resentments ultimately leading to the American Revolution War that started in 1775.[30]

With her supporters deceased or dispersed, Phillis' life started to become a struggle. She married John Peters in November 1778, with the war still raging around them.[31] The war prevented her from getting any more shipments of her book, *Poems On Various Subjects,* because of the embargo on items coming in from England. Selling her book would be a battle.

The ongoing war made publishing another book impossible, as in those days you had to rely on subscriptions to get a book published.[32] As Carretta explains, "[a]uthors traditionally acquired the necessary capital by either finding a wealthy and influential patron or selling the proposed book to subscribers who committed in advance to purchase copies of the book when it appeared. . . . Subscription was probably the only source of independent financial support available to Phillis Wheatley."[33] With a lack of patrons subscribing to purchase her books due to the hardship of the war, Phillis' dream of publishing a second book could not be realized.[34] Phillis had a publisher interested in the book but their efforts came to naught—her dream and the publisher's plan was indeed, " . . . front-page news in the October 30th, 1779 issue of the *Boston Evening Post and General Advertiser,* the newspaper produced by the intended publishers of the book. . . . The advertisement was repeated on November 6th, 27th, and also on December 4th, 11th, and 18th."[35] The advertisement did not bring in the support needed to see the book through to publication.

Unfortunately, poverty continued to take its toll on Phillis and her family. Phillis and John's first two children died as a result of the poor living conditions the family endured. John was repeatedly imprisoned for his debts, and was likely in prison in the winter of 1784 when, on December 5, 1784, Phillis Wheatley died. She was only 31. Her and John's third child, a son, died soon after. She is said to be buried with her son, in an unmarked grave at the old Granary Burial Ground.[36] But her life, and her work, memorialized in her poetry, continues on. That is what I know.

It's been an honour and privilege to work on this poetry collection about her life. As a person of colour she had so many obstacles in her way, and to publish a book of poetry and achieve her freedom were both victories on so many levels. As a woman of colour, she inspires me and gives me hope, guiding me as I face obstacles in this life. She helps me to continue. I will never forget that and thank her for her strength, fortitude, grace, perseverance, and courage. We can all learn from Phillis.

How did I first come to know Phillis? After I had finished my BA degree in sociology at the University of Alberta, I took English literature courses as electives. Professor Teresa Zackodnik taught the class focused on women's writing, on women who found themselves on the margins, especially women of colour. It was an inspiring class, and that's where I learned about Phillis. After that class I often thought about Phillis, and all the obstacles she overcame. Later, when it was time for me to write my creative writing thesis for my Master's degree in English literature, she came into my mind again.

I think she called to me. It was meant to be. It's been an inspiring and illuminating journey writing this poetry collection about her. She encourages me; her spirit is insisting that I do not give up—in any way, shape, or form.

There is an African saying: we all stand on the shoulders of our ancestors. I really believe that—those who went before us guide us. Those from the past and present are connected to us, and help to propel us into the future. There is a connection, there is a bridge, there is a circle. So we must learn from those who went before us, and keep going. This is what we have to do. We have to take this path, and put one foot in front of the other. This is what I know.

## NOTES

1   Vincent Carretta, *Phillis Wheatley: Biography of a Genius in Bondage* (Athens, GA: University of Georgia Press, 2014), 14–16.

2   Henry Louis Gates Jr., *The Trials of Phillis Wheatley: America's First Black Poet and Her Encounters with the Founding Fathers* (New York: Basic Civitas Books, 2003), 15.

3   Carretta, *Phillis Wheatley*, 65.

4   Amy L. Peters, "Fighting for Freedom: Slavery and New England" in *Cherished Possessions: A New England Legacy—Educator's Resource Guide*, (Boston: Society for the Preservation of New England Antiquities [SPNEA], 2003), 51.

5   "Edmund Quincy," Social Networks and Archival Context, accessed June 26, 2020, https://snaccooperative.org/ark:/99166/w6z03qh2; City of Andover, "Lest We Forget: Andover, and the Civil War," accessed June 26, 2020, https://www.andoverlestweforget.com/faces-of-andover/russell-whipple/edmund-quincy-2/; Library of Congress, "Today in History—November 7," accessed June 26, 2020, https://www.loc.gov/item/today-in-history/november-07/#:~:text=On%20November%207%2C%201837%2C%20Elijah,strengthened%20the%20cause%20of%20abolition.,

6   Matilda Odell, *Memoir and Poems of Phillis Wheatley* (Boston: Geo W. Light, 1834), accessed March 1, 2015 via *Documenting the American South* (Chapel Hill: University of North Carolina at Chapel Hill, 1999), http://docsouth.unc.edu/neh/wheatley/wheatley.html.

7   Carretta, *Phillis Wheatley*, 76–77; 91–93.

8   Carretta, *Phillis Wheatley*, 78.

9      Aaron Crossley Hobart Seymour, *Life and Times of Selina: Countess of Huntingdon, Volume 1,* edited by Jacob Kirkman Foster (London: William Edward Painter, 1844), 32–34, accessed via Google Books, https://books. google.ca/books?id=FI0yAQAAMAAJ&dq=Life+and+Times+of+Selina:+ Countess+of+Huntingdon,+Volume+1.; R. John Tyson, "Lady Huntingdon, Religion and Race," *Methodist History* 50, no.1 (2011): 28, 32. *Archives and History: The United Methodist Church.*

10     R. John Tyson, *Lady Huntingdon,* 38.

11     Vincent Carretta, *Phillis Wheatley: Complete Writings* (New York: Penguin Books, 2001), xvi.

12     Bill Hand, "When George Whitefield Came to Town," *Sun Journal: New Bern, North Carolina,* April 28, 2019, https://www.newbernsj.com/ news/20190428/when-george-whitefield-came-to-town#:~:text=George%20 Whitefield%20was%20a%20British,twice%E2%80%94in%201739% 20and%201764.; Christianity Today, "George Whitefield: Sensational Evangelist of Britain and America," accessed June 26, 2020, https://www. christianitytoday.com/history/people/evangelistsandapologists/george-whitefield.html.

13     Carretta, *Phillis Wheatley,* 75.

14     Carretta, *Phillis Wheatley,* 75.

15     Caretta, *Phillis Wheatley,* 76.

16     Caretta, *Phillis Wheatley,* 91-92; Caretta, *Complete Writings,* "Introduction," xvi.

17     Doak, Robin S., *Phillis Wheatley: Slave And Poet,* 38.

18     Carretta, *Phillis Wheatley,* 95, 109.

19     Carretta, *Phillis Wheatley,* 119.

20     Imtiaz Habib and Marika Sherwood, "Strong, Somerset and Sharp: Liberating Black Slaves in England," last modified September 29, 2009, https://archives.history.ac.uk/guildhallmanuscripts/strong.htm.

21     Habib and Sherwood, "Strong, Somerset and Sharp"; Carretta, *Phillis Wheatley,* 119, 120.

22     Carretta, *Phillis Wheatley,* 120–121.

23     Carretta, *Phillis Wheatley,* 121.

24     John C. Shields (ed), *Collected Works of Phillis Wheatley* (New York: Oxford University Press, 1988), 170; Robin S. Doak, *Phillis Wheatley: Slave and Poet,* 55.

25     Jeff Dacus, "Again the Hero: David Wooster's Final Battle," *Journal of the American Revolution,* June 19, 2018, https://allthingsliberty.com/2018/06/ again-the-hero-david-woosters-final-battle.

26    Mukhtar Ali Isani, "On the Death of General Wooster," Modern Philology, 77, no. 3 (1980): 307.

27    Isani, "On the Death of General Wooster," 307.

28    Isani, "On the Death of General Wooster," 308.

29    Edmund S. Morgan, "Thomas Hutchinson and the Stamp Act," *The New England Quarterly*, 21, no.4 (1948): 459–460; Carretta, *Phillis Wheatley*, 68.

30    Carretta, *Phillis Wheatley*, 68–74.

31    Carretta, *Phillis Wheatley*, 173.

32    Carretta, *Phillis Wheatley*, 94–95; Margaretta Matilda Odell, *Memoir and Poems*, 22–23; Emily R. Smith, *Phillis Wheatley*, 21.

33    Carretta, *Phillis Wheatley*, 82–83.

34    Odell, *Memoir and Poems*, 22–23.

35    Carretta, *Phillis Wheatley*, 178–179.

36    Vincent Carretta, "Was Phillis Wheatley's Husband A Crook Or A Dreamer?" Oxford University Press Blog, September, 2017, https://blog.oup.com/2017/02/john-peters-phillis-wheatley/; Carretta, *Phillis Wheatley*, 189–190.

# Bibliography

Carretta, Vincent. *Phillis Wheatley: Biography of a Genius in Bondage*. Athens, GA: University of Georgia Press, 2014.

———, ed. *Phillis Wheatley: Complete Writings*. New York: Penguin Books, 2001.

———, "Was Phillis Wheatley's Husband A Crook Or A Dreamer?" *Oxford University Press Blog*, September, 2017. https://blog.oup.com/2017/02/john-peters-phillis-wheatley/.

Christianity Today. "George Whitefield: Sensational Evangelist of Britain and America." Accessed June 27, 2020. https://www.christianitytoday.com/history/people/evangelistsandapologists/george-whitefield.html.

City of Andover. "Lest We Forget: Andover, and the Civil War." June 26, 2020. https://www.andoverlestweforget.com/faces-of-andover/russell-whipple/edmund-quincy-2/.

Dacus, Jeff. "Again the Hero: David Wooster's Final Battle." *Journal of the American Revolution*. June 19, 2018. https://allthingsliberty.com/2018/06/again-the-hero-david-woosters-final-battle.

Doak, Robin S. *Phillis Wheatley: Slave and Poet*. Minneapolis: Compass Point Books, 2006.

Gates, Henry Louis, Jr. *The Trials of Phillis Wheatley: America's First Black Poet and Her Encounters with the Founding Fathers*. New York: Basic Civitas Books, 2003.

Habib, Imtiaz and Marika Sherwood. "Strong, Somerset, and Sharp: Liberating Black Slaves in England." 24 June 2020. https:// https://archives.history.ac.uk/guildhallmanuscripts/strong.htm.

Hand, Bill. "When George Whitefield Came to Town." *Sun Journal: ew Bern, North Carolina*. April 28, 2019. https://www.newbernsj.com/news/20190428/when-george-whitefield-came-to-town#:~:text=George%20Whitefield%20was%20a%20British,twice%E2%80%94in%201739%20and%201764.

Isani, Mukhtar Ali. "On the Death of General Wooster." *Modern Philology* 77.3 (1980): 306-309. JSTOR.

Library of Congress. "Today in History—November 7: Elijah Lovejoy." Accessed June 26, 2020. https://www.loc.gov/item/today-in-history/november-07/#:~:text=On%20November%207%2C%20 1837%2C%20Elijah,strengthened%20the%20cause%20of%20 abolition.

Morgan, Edmund S. "Thomas Hutchinson and the Stamp Act." *The New England Quarterly,* 21.4 (1948): 459-492. JSTOR.

Odell, Margaretta M. *Memoir and Poems of Phillis Wheatley.* Boston: Geo W. Light, 1834. Accessed via *Documenting the American South.* University of North Carolina at Chapel Hill. 1999. http://docsouth. unc.edu/neh/wheatley/wheatley.html.

Peters, Amy L. *Cherished Possessions: A New England Legacy—Educator's Resource Guide.* Boston: Society for the Preservation of New England Antiquities (SPNEA), 2003. https://files.eric.ed.gov/ fulltext/ED481926.pdf.

Seymour, Aaron Crossley Hobart. *Life and Times of Selina: Countess of Huntingdon, Volume 1.* Edited by Jacob Kirkman Foster. London: William Edward Painter, 1844. Accessed via Google Books. https://books.google.ca/books?id=FI0yAQAAMAAJ&dq =Life+and+Times+of+Selina:+Countess+of+Huntingdon, +Volume+1.

Shields, John, ed. *The Collected Works of Phillis Wheatley.* New York: Oxford University Press, 1988.

Social Networks and Archival Context (SNAC). "Edmund Quincy." Accessed June 26, 2020. https://snaccooperative.org/ ark:/99166/w6z03qh2.

Smith, Emily R. *Phillis Wheatley.* Huntington Beach: Shell Education, 2004.

Tyson, John. R. "Lady Huntingdon, Religion and Race." *Methodist History* 50.1 (2011): 28-39. *Archives and History: The United Methodist Church.*

Wheatley, Phillis. *Phillis Wheatley: Complete Writings,* edited by Vincent Carretta. New York: Penguin Books, 2001.

Additional Resources

Moore, Geneva Cobb. *Maternal Metaphors of Power in African American Women's Literature: From Phillis Wheatley to Toni Morrison.* Columbia, SC: The University of South Carolina Press, 2017.

Shields, John C. *Phillis Wheatley and the Romantics.* Knoxville: The University of Tennessee Press, 2010.

Wheatley, Phillis. *Poems on Various Subjects, Religious and Moral.* London: A. Bell, 1773.

# Acknowledgements

There were many instrumental people who guided me on this journey. I have to thank University of Calgary Press and Aritha van Herk for giving me the opportunity to bring the world of Phillis Wheatley to the printed page. Helen Hajnoczky, I thank you for understanding and sharing my vision, your intuitive suggestions and insight. I must mention and thank Melina Cusano who did the beautiful cover design of the book.

I also thank Amanda Cockrell, my creative writing thesis supervisor for *Phillis*, Hillary Homzie, my second reader, and all other supportive spirits from Hollins University. I remember and give thanks to Teresa Zackodnik, from the University Of Alberta, who introduced me to Phillis.

I also give thanks to Adriana Davies, who guided me on this journey, as well as T.D.L. Turner and Linda Harrison. Other supportive spirits include Amanda Lim for her feedback and encouragement. Pierrette Requier, you are a Guiding Light. Joan Crate, you inspire me.

I also would like to thank Sean Baker, Yang Lim, Nadia Sadi, Yvonne Aldred, Sandra Quimiro, Susanne Goshko, Barb F. Schweger, Shawnna and John Pracejus, Loann Gordon, Renée Gittens, all of the Jordans, including Gloria Jordan, Stan Jordan, Darren, and Rose.

For their never-ending support, I would also like to mention Carol Holmes, the rest of the WGA, the Stroll of Poets, Parkland Poets, Rachel Figeys, Cecilia Wyand, Jacqueline Williams, Stephanie Ann Foster, Kelly Canner Pocano, Kris Stultz, Elsa Robinson, Tololwa Mollel, Odion Welch, Taneya Rogers, Greg Davis, Nigel Williams, Nilo Adinkrahene,

Amanda Nothando, Tracy Folorunsho-Barry, Osas Oweka-Smith, Shirley Romany, Jean Romany, Kiana Johnson-Laing, Jo-anne Wong, Deanna Chou, Tee Adeyemo, Sherry Skinner, Rose Brophy O'Neill, Michael Broodhagen, Tatiana Lissov Kastner, Harriet Tinka, Frankline Agbor, Gisele Ndoungo, Pippa and Michael Dovey.

I would like to thank those who were also inspirational as I stepped into the world of Phillis Wheatley: Amanda Blunt, Evan Blunt, Eileen Bell, BD Wilson, Ruby Swekla, Bonnie Knoll, Gilmore and Joy Hurst, Anton Thomas, Robbie Austin, Calvin Austin, Eunice Carter, Evette Layne-Linton, Melissa Conlon, Rebecca John, Toya Richardson, Annet Maitwe, Twilla Coates, Shanelle Ceretzke, Joy Thomas, Constance Thomas, Barb Murray, Jana Pocrjna, Dolly Gabat, and Dorothy Drummond.

I would also like to remember all the Carters, including the family in Jamaica, along with shining spirits like Inez Callum. All the Clarkes in Alberta are a supportive force, including Alston and Anita Clarke, Nell Marshall, Amorette Bradshaw, Sara Gabriel, and James Clarke.

I also would like to thank all the Clarkes in the United Kingdom: Reg, Val, Ada, Hiram, Jacqui, and Natalie. Louise Rhule, Parnell Rhule, Ann Bain, Maz Rhone, Hyacinth and Katrina Campbell, Adrian Mayers, Steve Wood, Doreen Wood, Ian and Janet Ellis have also supported me on my artistic path. They are also part of the family from the United Kingdom. I also would like to thank all of the Duggans who are a shining light.

There are many people who are also a part of my artistic journey. To everyone—I thank you for your encouragement and support.

ALISON CLARKE is an award winning author and poet. She holds a Master's degree in Children's literature from Hollins University. Alison is the author of *The Sisterhood Series*. She won the 2016 Writer Of The Year award from *Diversity Magazine* for *The Sisterhood: Book One*, a novel about Oppie, a sorceress' daughter, and her best friend who is a dragon, and the journey they go on to save the universe. In *The Sisterhood Series* are themes of the power of the Collective force, the power of art, and featuring girls and women, especially those of colour as protagonists.

Alison is also an award winning visual artist. Her paintings of her characters have been featured at the Art Gallery of Alberta, the University of Alberta, at an art show in Roanoke, Virginia, and at other art shows in her home of Edmonton and internationally.

Alison believes that all forms of art—literary, visual, and so on—can change the world. Being a writer-in-residence at the Lotus Art Gallery, from September to December 2016, and teaching creative writing classes as part of her residency, was an inspiring experience for Alison. She has also taught creative writing and visual art through other various organizations.

Alison also enjoys performing spoken word, and has been a performer at Black Arts Matter, a festival in Edmonton featuring black spoken word artists, as well as other local events.

Travelling to festivals around the world has also captivated Alison, as she believes that travelling is magical and mystical. She has been to conventions in London, England, meeting authors from around the world who write in various genres such as fantasy or science fiction. Alison has done readings, book signings, and writing workshops at various conventions and festivals, including Edge Lit 8 in Derby, England. She enjoys meeting people, and talking about the magic of story.

# BRAVE & BRILLIANT SERIES

SERIES EDITOR:
Aritha van Herk, Professor, English, University of Calgary
ISSN 2371-7238 (PRINT) ISSN 2371-7246 (ONLINE)

Brave & Brilliant encompasses fiction, poetry, and everything in between and beyond. Bold and lively, each with its own strong and unique voice, Brave & Brilliant books entertain and engage readers with fresh and energetic approaches to storytelling and verse, in print or through innovative digital publication.